Discover Joy

Discover Joy

Well-Being, God's Way

Dr. Joy Bodzioch

www.dpibooks.org

Discover Joy

©2009 by DPI Books
5016 Spedale Court #331
Spring Hill, TN 37174

All rights reserved.
No part of this book may be duplicated, copied, translated, reproduced or stored mechanically or electronically without specific, written permission of Discipleship Publications International.

All Scripture quotations, unless indicated, are taken from the NEW INTERNATIONAL VERSION.
Copyright ©1973, 1978, 1984 by the International Bible Society.
Used by permission of Zondervan Publishing House.
All rights reserved.

Scripture quotations marked NLT are taken from the Holy Bible, New Living Translation, copyright 1996, 2004.
Used by permission of Tyndale House Publishers, Inc., Wheaton, Illinois 60189. All rights reserved.

The "NIV" and "New International Version" trademarks are registered in the United States Patent Trademark Office by the International Bible Society.
Use of either trademarks requires the permission of the International Bible Society.

Printed in the United States of America

Cover Design: Brian Branch
Interior Design: Thais Gloor
Cover image: ©iStockphoto.com/aleaimage

Shell drawing on page 27: Davin Iyamatsu

ISBN: 978-1-57782-236-3

With much love, to my four favorite guys:

My wonderful husband, Adam—
you must have been created just for me!

My son, Greg—
you inspired me to become a disciple of Jesus!

My grandsons, Brandon and Cameron—
this is my legacy for you!

CONTENTS

Discover Joy

Reflecting on how this book came to be, I'm amazed at God's gracious intervention and miraculous work in the lives of ordinary people who are simply willing to step out in faith. Although this book feels like a culmination of my life's work, in reality it's much more than that. To me, *Discover Joy* is a personal demonstration of 2 Corinthians 12:9: God's power made perfect in my weakness!

God must have planned it all along, but humanly speaking it all began when my parents combined their names to create mine—"J" from Jean and "oy" from Roy—to come up with Joy. Family life in our home was pretty typical: no real abuse but lots of dysfunction. Mother and Dad were dealing with their own life challenges, and although I don't doubt they did their best, my memories of growing up are far from joyful.

An only child (until my early teens), I remember feeling very much alone. When asked as a tot if I had any brothers or sisters, I responded, "No. I'm a lonely child." My parents liked to chuckle about my cute mispronunciation of "only," but as an adult I realized it had actually been true.

Sometime in that awkward preteen period, I overheard my parents say they had once thought I was especially intelligent, but then realized I was average. Laughing, they said they had decided to put their hopes in my little sister. (Years later I asked them about this, and they vehemently denied it, but what I *believed* they had said powerfully shaped my self-worth.)

By my late teens I struggled with tremendous insecurity. During a piano recital my hands shook so violently that I began my performance three times and finally dissolved in tears, running from the auditorium. This was especially humiliating because I was the oldest—and most advanced—of the students, and my parents and boyfriend were in the audience!

Despite all this, God was working. My parents weren't especially religious, but a mustard seed of faith had somehow been planted in my heart and nurtured. At thirteen I attended a weekend Bible retreat, and at sixteen heard Billy Graham speak during a crusade in Philadelphia. I dedicated my life to Christ, having no idea what that really meant but wanting to follow him nevertheless.

I can relate to the Israelites, since I spent the next forty years wandering and struggling in my personal "desert." I knew a lot of folks who were really trying to live by the Bible, but they often did not seem to find happiness or contentment any more easily than others who didn't profess faith in God. For me, the Big Question was, "Since God clearly wants to give us a life full of joy, where is the concise, step-by-step plan for achieving it?"

Just as God has always taken care of his people, throughout my time in the desert, he was constantly faithful, guiding and encouraging and inspiring me despite my doubts and disobedience. I considered myself a Christian and had enjoyed a relationship with God since my teens, but I had to admit that my life wasn't a great example of New Testament Christianity. So I asked some women in our church to teach me more about the Bible, and I was baptized into Christ in 1994.

Almost exactly ten years later, during my daily Bible study, I finally found the treasure—God's perfect plan for true well-being!

Like a man who stumbles upon a buried treasure, at first I did not appreciate what I had found. That day I happened to be studying the fifth chapter of Matthew, comparing various translations and commentaries. Although I had read the Beatitudes many times, suddenly I saw that Jesus was actually telling us how to be happy or joyful. Somehow, it seemed significant that these were the first words of Jesus' first sermon in the first book of the New Testament.

I grew more and more excited as I grasped that this might be the answer that had eluded me—and best of all, it was summarized right there in just a few verses. This was good news! But there was bad news too: these verses weren't all that easy to interpret. What did Jesus mean by "poor in spirit" or being "meek"?

Over the next few weeks, the more I studied it, the more I realized this passage seemed to encapsulate or relate to other well-known scriptures. Little by little, I began to truly understand what Jesus was saying, and to test it in my own life. When I was feeling discouraged or frustrated or anxious, I would ask which of these verses was *not* true of my character.

Once I saw that I had found a reliable spiritual guide, I considered what steps I could take to grow in the various heart qualities Jesus was describing. As a psychologist, many of my colleagues and clients had complained that their lives were *just okay*, that they still felt they were missing out on that passion for life or vibrant sense of well-being which is supposed to be part of "the good life." Since I had not yet discovered the secret for myself, I had not been able to share it with them either.

Eventually I saw that the reason these beatitudes lead to real joy is that they are in fact the introduction to life in the kingdom of God—life lived out here in this world under the reign of God.

I began to write and quickly completed three chapters of a new book: *Discover Joy.* Then, as happens, *life* intervened and the manuscript sat untouched for three years. But by 2007 I developed a conviction that God was calling me to complete what I (or *he)* had begun.

My husband, Adam, agreed that I should seek work in a more supportive environment where I'd have the physical and emotional energy to work on the book. With seven chapters remaining, my goal was to finish it in a little over a year.

Once employed in my new position, I attacked the project with renewed energy, writing each morning for an hour before work. Armed with my Bible, an outline and much prayer, in amazement I experienced God's gracious response. Without fail, day after day he poured the words into my mind, so that by the end of four months the manuscript was complete!

How can you benefit from this book? First of all, this is a "learn-by-doing book" rather than just a "good read." Chapters 2–9 include a section entitled "For More Reflection," which follows each step in the process of developing the characteristic Jesus is describing. Please don't skip over these if you want to reap the reward! Purchase a notebook and use it to complete the exercises.

Even better, find a partner or small group who will join you in this spiritual quest. Make a commitment to read and work through the exercises, one chapter per month or every two weeks, meeting together to discuss what you're learning and encourage each other as you overcome any challenges you may face along the way.

I'm so excited to share what I'm learning with you! The one thing of which I'm one-hundred-percent certain is that God is true to his word. The more we obey him, not out of duty but out of love, the more he will enrich and bless our lives, and fill our hearts with his peace and contentment—his *joy!*

Much love in Him,
Joy Bodzioch
January 2009

Note: The names of people cited in examples have been changed.

1

The Search for Joy

But the angel said to them, "Do not be afraid. I bring you good news of great joy that will be for all the people."

Luke 2:10

In 1974, as a fledgling decorator, I established a business called Joy of Living Interiors—JOLI for short. More than a play on my name, this business represented my dream to discover for myself and others the keys to experiencing real fulfillment—joy—on a daily basis. Although I had tried to follow Jesus for fourteen years, I still felt something was missing. I was not suffering from depression or any actual "disorder," but the full life Jesus promised in John 10:10 seemed beyond my reach.

Jesus came to bring us joy. But how many of us can truthfully say that we are filled with joy, regardless of our circumstances? What about you? Are you able to "rejoice in the Lord always" (Philippians 4:4)?

Christians should be more joyful than nonbelievers. This is clear because we see that the Scriptures are infused with joy. When you include all the forms of "joy" and "rejoice" in the New International Version, there are more than four hundred references. God gives us everything we need for life and godliness (2 Peter 1:3), so this means he also gives us the ability to be joyful.

I believe that my name is no accident, and that God gave me a personal mission: to discover and share his secrets for experiencing joy on a consistent basis. This information is what I needed to learn myself, as is typical of most teachers, and it is what I hope to pass on to you through this book.

In the 1980s I became a psychologist, hoping to find the keys to joy. But I soon discovered that psychology did not have the answers either. God promises "seek and you will find" (Matthew 7:7), and although I wandered in the "desert of confusion" for forty years, I finally found the answers I was searching for. Why don't we begin at the beginning?

A Great Human Quest

> After much thought, I decided to cheer myself with wine. And while still seeking wisdom, I clutched at foolishness. In this way, I tried to experience the only happiness most people find during their brief life in this world. (Ecclesiastes 2:3, NLT)

God created you and me with a desire to know and be one with him. Paul described the result or "fruit" of this oneness with God's Spirit as "love, joy, peace, patience, kindness, goodness, faithfulness, gentleness and self-control" (Galatians 5:22–23). This is the emptiness we long to fill, the state we desire to achieve—we generally call it "happiness."

I call it "vibrant mental health" because it is where we find inner peace and contentment—freedom from worry, insecurity, anxiety, depression, guilt and fear.

Sound too good to be true?

That is because, for most of us, this blissful state flits in and out of our lives like a butterfly, giving us a momentary glimpse, a taste, just a sense of what could be, if only…

The danger is that our lives can become a series of "if onlys"—if only I had a bigger house, a better marriage, a higher paying job. If only I could lose weight, get along with so-and-so, finish my degree. If only I had this or could do that, then I would be happy.

Of course, the healthy way to respond to "if onlys" is to turn them into goals, and at the same time to recognize that worldly pursuits will not really determine our happiness in the long term.

The privileged, who are not struggling just to survive, eventually realize that this emptiness signals a dissatisfaction. But because of a distaste for "organized religion," they may end up thrill-seeking in all the wrong places. I think this explains why horror movies score at the box office and why many of our TV shows are either sexually charged or explore the occult with ghosts, mediums or vampires. People are looking for something outside themselves to fill up their emptiness.

The good news is that Jesus left us a treasure map! This map contains concise directions for finding vibrant mental health, all summarized in one biblical passage. These instructions clearly show which way to go and light the path to the life of joy that Jesus came to bring. And when our lives are off course or stuck in a rut, when our tires are sinking into depression or our tank is high on anxiety and low on faith, we have a perfect "diagnostic tool" for getting back on track.

Do you know where to find this treasure map? Yes, it is in the Bible, but can you turn to it? Try telling someone who has expressed an interest in learning about Christianity that the Bible is God's instruction manual for fulfilling their destiny. They are likely to give you the same look I would if you handed me an engine repair manual and told me to go fix my car.

The truth is that life travelers—even those who are consciously seeking the joy of God as their destination—benefit from some additional travel guides. This book is intended to be such a guide.

The Route to Self-Fulfillment

> "What good is it for a man to gain the whole world, and yet lose or forfeit his very self?" (Luke 9:25)

For several years, as a speaker and seminar leader, I had believed and taught that an experience of joy came from becoming fully and uniquely yourself: Just One You! This idea was appealing but the question was still "How do people become fully themselves?" I had to admit that the six-step "UNIQUE" program I had developed seemed superficial and did not really help those whose self-worth had been damaged by traumatic experiences.[1]

Even more troubling, there seemed to be no biblical support for the idea that we could achieve joy by becoming fully ourselves. Instead, the Bible said clearly that we achieve joy by emptying and denying ourselves. Philippians, the most "joyful" book in the Bible, was written while Paul was in prison. Jesus taught that we find life through self-denial (Matthew 16:24–27), and the psalmist said that those who "sow in tears will reap with songs of joy" (Psalm 126:5).

Finally, since the Bible "fully equips us" (2 Timothy 3:17), it did not make sense to me that God would have left the details for achieving joy out of his book.

Spirituality and Mental Health

"My purpose is to give them a rich and satisfying life." (John 10:10, NLT)

God is the joy expert! But as middle-class Americans have increasingly sought more from life than mere survival, psychologists have inevitably gotten into the act. Thus the search often begins, not with a discussion of joy, but of "self-actualization" and mental health.

In 1946 the World Health Organization had defined "health" as a "state of complete physical, mental, and social well-being, not merely the absence of disease and infirmity."[2] But in reality psychologists were focused mostly on the "disease" while ignoring the ways to promote "physical, mental and social well-being."

Eventually, researchers began to talk about mental health, which they described as having three components: suffering, function and coherence. "Health" was defined as the absence of suffering, along with the presence of function (ability to function normally). Coherence was a sense of inner peace and predictability (even with little controllability), along with the optimistic outlook that things will work out reasonably well.

To me, this sounds like faith, although people credit this experience of coherence to many other things besides a relationship with God. Others called this third quality "hardiness" or "resilience."[3]

Next, psychologists identified six aspects of psychological well-being:

- Self-acceptance (positive attitudes toward yourself)
- Personal growth (a feeling of continued development)
- Purpose in life (life goals and a sense of direction)
- Environmental mastery (competence to manage life's responsibilities)
- Autonomy (confidence in one's own opinions)
- Positive relations with others.[4]

There were also five dimensions of social well-being:

- Social acceptance (positive attitudes toward people)
- Social actualization (believing society can progress in a positive direction)
- Social contribution (understanding your own potential to make a contribution)
- Social coherence (seeing the world as logical and predictable)
- Social integration (feeling a part of your community)[5]

Most exciting, though, is the fact that psychologists like Ken Pargament and Annette Mahoney finally acknowledged the existence of God and began to consider spirituality an important research topic in mental health. They also claimed that "the capacity to envision, seek, connect and hold on to, and transform the sacred may be what makes us uniquely human."[6]

Some of these fascinating studies have shown that

- Religious involvement is associated with increased health and decreased mental and physical illness.[7]
- Striving to achieve goals related to an ultimate purpose or commitment to a higher power may result in greater well-being than striving for other types of goals.[8]
- People who experience God as loving, compassionate and responsive report higher levels of well-being than people who describe him as distant, harsh or punishing.[9]
- People in crisis who do not maintain a positive view of God are at greater risk for mental disorders.[10]
- Married couples who perceive their marriage as a divine calling or commitment tend to experience greater marital satisfaction, more investment in the marriage, less marital conflict, and more effective marital problem solving.[11]
- Parents who perceive that their role is God-given report being less verbally aggressive and more consistent in discipline with their children.[12]

Although this research does not necessarily define spirituality in biblical terms, it is important because, for the first time, we have begun to bridge the vast chasm between science and the validity of a personal relationship with the living God.

Similarities Between Descriptions of Well-Being?

Another interesting question remains: what, if any, are the similarities between descriptions of well-being contained in Scripture and in the writings of non-Christian mental health professionals?

In his book *Psychology, Theology, and Spirituality in Christian Counseling*,[13] Mark McMinn describes how Paul's fruits of the Spirit found in Galatians 5 are similar to the characteristics and desires of self-actualizers described by humanistic psychologist Abraham Maslow:

Fruit of the Spirit	Characteristic: Self-Actualizers	Desires: Self-Actualizers
Love	Profound relationships	Unity, beauty
Joy	Spontaneity, peak experiences, Continued freshness of appreciation	Aliveness, playfulness
Peace	Fellowship with humanity, Acceptance of self and others	Simplicity
Patience		Individuality, richness
Kindness	Unhostile sense of humor	Justice
Goodness	Efficient perception of reality	Goodness, values, truth
Faithfulness		Completion
Gentleness		Balance, harmony
Self-control	Autonomy, task-centeredness	

Of course, just because the above results look similar does not necessarily mean that psychotherapy and Christian spirituality have the same goals. At the same time, the above information does demonstrate that, although some might claim that psychology has cornered the market on the benefits of "self-actualization," the Bible was showing us how to achieve this joyful state almost 2000 years before a science of human behavior even existed.

Finding Joy, God's Way

> Rejoice in the Lord always. I will say it again: Rejoice! Let your gentleness be evident to all. The Lord is near. (Philippians 4:4–5)

Paul's advice to the Christians in Philippi reminds me of something my husband, Adam, says. He likes to quote the wisdom of his grandfather: "Easy to say—hard to do!" Most would agree that to rejoice always is one of the more difficult biblical commands to practice. Nevertheless, the experience of joy is an earmark of vibrant mental health, and it's within our reach when we follow Jesus' biblical roadmap.

Much of the Bible is clear and straightforward, but when we seek the truth through deeper study, God rewards our effort with wisdom that goes beyond the obvious. This definitely applies to the Bible's directives for experiencing joy.

What about the difference between joy and happiness? "Happy" is one of those words we use daily but, like "love," it seems to have lost much of its original meaning. Joy is more than simple momentary happiness. Two Greek words—*makarios* and *chara*—are often used in the New Testament to describe happiness.

According to Zondervan's *Exhaustive Concordance*, *makarios* refers to being "blessed (receiving God's favor), good (in a position of favor), happy (feelings associated with receiving God's favor)," while *chara* means "joy, rejoicing, happiness, gladness." Putting the definitions of these two words together, I find that joy is more like contentment, an abiding conviction that "all things do work together for good" (Romans 8:28), regardless of difficult circumstances.

In his book, *Authentic Happiness*, psychologist Martin Seligman makes the following observation:

> The belief that we can rely on shortcuts to happiness, joy, rapture, comfort, and ecstasy, rather than be entitled to these feelings by the exercise of personal strengths and virtues, leads to legions of people who in the middle of great wealth are starving spiritually. Positive emotion alienated from the exercise of character leads to emptiness, to inauthenticity, to depression and, as we age, to the gnawing realization that we are fidgeting until we die.[14]

Seligman seems to consider character the essential element in experiencing happiness. This brings to mind James' teaching:

> But the man who looks intently into the perfect law that gives freedom, and continues to do this, not forgetting what he has heard, but doing it—he will be blessed in what he does. (James 1:25)

Although happiness and joy are similar, in the Bible happiness most often results from outward circumstances, while joy reflects a sense of inward well-being. Since joy is a fruit of God's Spirit, we might wonder whether true joy would even be available to the non-Christian. Whatever the answer, as God's children we are not only able to experience joy, but living God's way should also bring us more positive circumstances—happiness—since the Bible shows us how to have harmonious relationships, be productive employees, avoid addictions and more.

Throughout the rest of this book, we will focus on finding joy, assuming that a joyful state will also bring happiness (whereas the reverse may not always be true).

Who Needs 'Vibrant Mental Health'?

> If your law hadn't sustained me with joy, I would have died in my misery. I will never forget your commandments, for by them you give me life. (Psalm 119:92–93, NLT)

With the psalmist, I believe that

- God's word is the key to experiencing—and sustaining—an experience of joy (vibrant mental health)
- At times we will feel sick or unhappy, but remaining in Christ—the living word—enables us to overcome
- When we neglect our mental or physical health, the Scriptures can help restore us to peak condition

This does not mean that a Christian should never see a mental health professional or use appropriate medications. However, I do believe that many who suffer with emotional challenges like anxiety and depression would benefit by first facing their spiritual crisis. When we rush to a therapist to "talk out" or "medicate away" the pain, we may be robbing ourselves of God's signals that, when we do not follow his instruction book and the loving help of Christian friends, our lives simply will not function as designed.

In addition, the goal of psychotherapy is increased self-esteem and self-reliance, which is actually at cross-purposes with God's plan. As Dr. Charles Solomon puts it:

> Psychotherapy helps a person to meet his own needs; to learn more effective ways of thinking, feeling, and behaving; and to develop more adequate defense mechanisms. What the person may be missing is the truth Christ spoke: "Without me ye can do nothing" (John 15:5).
>
> As self (or ego, as Freud would define it) grows stronger, there is an increase in pride and a decrease in humility and dependence upon God.[15]

If you have personally found professional counseling to be beneficial, great! Nevertheless, I encourage everyone to consider the question, "Can I grow to be more joyful and more filled with *every* fruit of God's Spirit? Can I experience more of that full life Jesus described?"

Whether you are in the midst of an emotional crisis or simply want to grow, the following chapters are designed to inspire you "to know this love that surpasses knowledge—that you may be filled to the measure of all the fullness of God" (Ephesians 3:19).

Growing in Godliness

> Like newborn babies, crave pure spiritual milk, so that by it you may grow up in your salvation, now that you have tasted that the Lord is good. (1 Peter 2:2–3)

"Simply wanting to grow" actually turns out to be a very important goal; in fact, spiritual growth is not optional if we want to enjoy God's fullness. Jesus showed how growth is part of God's natural plan (Mark 4:26–29), and the psalmist reflected on how we can continue to blossom despite advancing age:

> The righteous will flourish like a palm tree,
> they will grow like a cedar of Lebanon;
> planted in the house of the LORD,
> they will flourish in the courts of our God.
> They will still bear fruit in old age,
> they will stay fresh and green. (Psalm 92:12–14)

In his classic devotional book, *Growing Spiritually,* E. Stanley Jones makes the point that God made us to grow spiritually, and like all living things, there are only two choices—growth or decay. He goes on to say,

> This decay of the person causes more unhappiness than all other causes combined. All other causes are marginal; this is central. For to know, consciously or unconsciously, that the central purpose of your being—the thing for which you are made—is unfulfilled, or worse, is being violated, is to cause a central and fundamental unhappiness to settle at the very center of your being.[16]

While it is true that finding joy in spiritual growth will result in greater life satisfaction and contentment, our motive is not selfish; the fact is that God commands it! Psalm 37:4 says to "delight yourself in the LORD, and he will give you the desires of your heart." God is pleased when we find joy in him. Remember, Jesus came to give us life "to the full" (John 10:10). That brings us to the essential question: how do we begin?

God's Guide to Vibrant Mental Health

> Now when he saw the crowds, he went up on a mountainside and sat down. His disciples came to him, and he began to teach them, saying:
>
> "Blessed are the poor in spirit,
> for theirs is the kingdom of heaven.
> Blessed are those who mourn,

> for they will be comforted.
> Blessed are the meek,
> for they will inherit the earth.
> Blessed are those who hunger and thirst for righteousness,
> for they will be filled.
> Blessed are the merciful,
> for they will be shown mercy.
> Blessed are the pure in heart,
> for they will see God.
> Blessed are the peacemakers,
> for they will be called sons of God.
> Blessed are those who are persecuted because of righteousness,
> for theirs is the kingdom of heaven.
>
> "Blessed are you when people insult you, persecute you and falsely say all kinds of evil against you because of me. Rejoice and be glad, because great is your reward in heaven, for in the same way they persecuted the prophets who were before you." (Matthew 5:1–12)

Christ's longest and most famous sermon, recorded early in Matthew, begins with this passage known as the "Beatitudes." This word is not actually used in the scripture; the name comes from the fact that Jesus is describing how to be blessed by God. The word, "beatitude" comes from the Latin word for "blessed." Jesus is really talking about how to live at the very center of God's will.

Take a moment now to go back and read Matthew 5:1–12. What is your reaction to this passage? I recall how puzzling I found these verses. First, they just didn't seem logical: being poor, mourning and being persecuted did not sound very "blessed" to me! And then, reading them would leave me feeling discouraged—if God expected me to be this way, how could I ever measure up?

This certainly did not sound like the loving God I believed in! At some point I reasoned that the promised blessings would be provided in heaven (verse 12), but that they did not have much to do with feeling blessed during this life.

Then one day I discovered that some Bible translations substitute the word "happy" for "blessed" (*makarios* in the Greek), and I decided to study the Beatitudes more closely. If this was Christ's guide to happiness, I wanted to learn more.

I should also mention that I came to believe the Beatitudes are progressive steps—we cannot skip over one, two and three to take step four (as I might have wished). Only when we have taken (or at least begun to take) the "lower" steps are we ready for the "higher" steps. The *Thompson Chain Reference Bible*, in fact, visually portrays the Sermon on the Mount as a "temple of truth" in which the Beatitudes form the foundation—eight progressive steps by which men reach the higher altitudes of spiritual life.[17]

In his book, *The Beatitudes for Today,* James C. Howell says:

> At least as far back as the fourth century, theologians (such as Gregory of Nyssa) imagined the complete set of Beatitudes as a staircase, ascending toward God. For Jesus, the eight Beatitudes are not like the high school quiz in which "only four of these eight need be attempted in the allotted time." We will see how the poor in spirit are compelled to mourn, how the meek hunger for righteousness, how the pure in heart are merciful, and therefore they strive to make peace, and wind up being hassled because of it.[18]

As my study progressed, I began to suspect a fascinating relationship between these concepts and other key scriptures. First, the passage in Matthew 5 appears to provide instruction for growing in Paul's fruit of the Spirit. It also turns out that chapters 18–20 of Matthew, where Christ teaches the principles of his kingdom, contain many of the same ideas as the Beatitudes, presented in a similar order.

Finally, I realized that these teachings seem to encapsulate the most important principles contained in both Old and New

Testaments! They show us how to live life on this earth by the kingdom values that Jesus came to give us. This began an exciting adventure—a treasure hunt to unearth the secrets I had been searching for. But this is not a journey to take alone, so I invite you to join me! Together we will embark on a path where, with faith, God will "do immeasurably more than all we ask or imagine, according to his power that is at work within us" (Ephesians 3:20).

My hope is that this book will be a springboard for your personal Bible study, leading you to even greater revelations and a closer walk with our wonderful Savior.

To conclude this section, here are "coming attractions" for the rest of the book:

Chapter 2	Decide to Be Wholehearted
Chapter 3	Imagine God's Comfort
Chapter 4	Surrender to God
Chapter 5	Commit to Spiritual Growth
Chapter 6	Overflow with Compassion
Chapter 7	Value Holiness
Chapter 8	Encourage Reconciliation
Chapter 9	Reflect the Heart of Christ
Chapter 10	Now Taste the Spirit's Fruit

Even as a little girl I was fascinated by seashells. One day as I contemplated how to portray the spiritual transformation in finding the joy of Christ, I was delighted to discover that the chambered nautilus is a perfect analogy for the progression from spiritual poverty (Matthew 5:3) to a sacrificial spirit (Matthew 5:10). (See figure 1.)

Starting at the widest section near the entrance to the shell, we "*Decide to Be Wholehearted,*" beginning our journey with God.

Moving inward, we then "*Imagine God's Comfort,*" as we acknowledge and mourn the impact of our sin. Next, we "*Surrender to God,*" turning our lives over to his control. Longing for intimacy with God, we "*Commit to Spiritual Growth*" and "*Overflow with Compassion*" by developing his heart of mercy. Imitating Jesus, for the first time we truly "*Value Holiness*" and move on to become peacemakers who can "*Encourage Reconciliation*" with God and other people.

Finally, exchanging our will for his we "*Reflect the Heart of Christ.*" Notice how the "path" narrows as we become more and more Christlike (Matthew 7:13–14) and how the final step in our progression is adjacent to the "heart" of the shell.

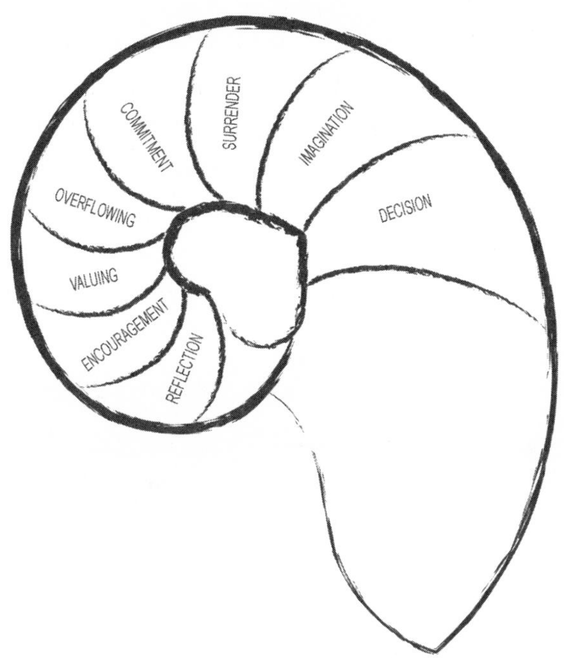

2

Spiritual Poverty

Decide to Be Wholehearted

"Blessed are the poor in spirit,
for theirs is the kingdom of heaven."
Matthew 5:3

Most of us feel happy in the best of times. When we experience good health, career success, financial security and harmonious relationships, we can convince ourselves that "this is the good life." If we were really honest, though, many of us would admit that even at these moments something often seems to be missing.

During my years in private practice, I often heard clients complain of an emptiness deep down inside and of a gnawing suspicion that, even during the pleasant times, they knew this peaceful experience wouldn't last long. Back then I could listen and provide psychological solutions and encouragement, but I had no spiritual answers. Now I remember those hurting people, knowing that I could have truly given them "living water" had I known then what I know now!

God wants us to have wonderful, fulfilling lives, but he also wants us to realize that something is wrong when we are not following his plan. Worldly pleasures may bring temporary self-esteem, but they are not the basis of a meaningful life.

Being able to discover joy even in difficult or painful circumstances is the objective of this book. Although God wills that we be filled with joy, he always gives us a choice. We can choose sin or righteousness (Romans 6:16), and according to Proverbs 10:28, "the prospect of the righteous is joy."

Throughout this book I will be wearing two hats: that of a psychologist whose purpose it is to provide the keys to vibrant mental health, and that of a disciple of Jesus who has learned (and is still learning) that life works best when I do it God's way. So let's embark on the most exhilarating adventure of our lives—a treasure hunt to discover the keys to God's blessing!

Shocking Truth from Jesus

As he often did, Jesus undoubtedly shocked the disciples that day as he spoke to them on the Mount of Olives. He began by telling them that being "poor in spirit" is a blessed state. Many of his listeners surely knew what poverty was like—and never considered it a blessing. Just imagine them looking at each other, wondering aloud what he was talking about. Maybe you are wondering the same thing.

Note that Jesus is not talking about physical poverty. He uses the term "poor in spirit." He is talking about spiritual poverty. What is spiritual poverty, and who has it?

Here are three steps that I believe can help us not only understand the meaning of spiritual poverty, but also to get to the place of blessing that Jesus described:

- Be Humble: Realize that "I can do nothing truly worthwhile on my own."
- Be Desperate: Acknowledge that "I don't have the power to change. I desperately need God's help—only God can heal me."
- Be Eager: Consciously choose to eagerly seek God and believe that "if I keep trusting God and seeking his way, I will find the fullness of life that he promises."

As a result, we…

Decide to Be Wholehearted

Step 1: Be Humble

> To some who were confident of their own righteousness and looked down on everybody else, Jesus told this parable: "Two men went up to the temple to pray, one a Pharisee and the other a tax collector. The Pharisee stood up and prayed about himself: 'God, I thank you that I am not like other men—robbers, evildoers, adulterers—or even like this tax collector. I fast twice a week and give a tenth of all I get.'
>
> "But the tax collector stood at a distance. He would not even look up to heaven, but beat his breast and said, 'God, have mercy on me, a sinner.'
>
> "I tell you that this man, rather than the other, went home justified before God. For everyone who exalts himself will be humbled, and he who humbles himself will be exalted." (Luke 18:9–14)

If there was one thing Jesus disliked, it was self-righteousness, and repenting of this sin is the goal of step one. The above parable recorded by Luke sheds light on the kind of humility valued by Jesus. A few verses later, Jesus tells the disciples that "anyone who will not receive the kingdom of God like a little child will never enter it" (Luke 18:17). In other words, we will only be rewarded with his kingdom if we have the humility of a child, the sense that we do not know what we are doing.

At the beginning of his reign, Solomon exemplified this kind of humility:

> "Now, O LORD my God, you have made your servant king in place of my father David. But I am only a little child and do not know how to carry out my duties." (1 Kings 3:7)

Desire to Change

I have seen many examples of people who come for counseling, but are not willing to change. "Beth" and "Charles" came to me with a troubled marriage. After less than a year together, Charles complained of "incompatible" needs and expectations, and like many other husbands, he agreed to counseling only when Beth told him *she* needed help. Unfortunately, although these men often admit their own unhappiness once in the counseling situation, Charles was unwilling to acknowledge the pain he felt or admit his need to change.

Despite two previous divorces, he simply stated that marrying Beth was a mistake which could only be rectified by going their separate ways. If Charles remained unwilling to "humble out," he and Beth would never be able to resolve their differences and achieve a harmonious and satisfying relationship. He was great at intellectualizing, but healing happens in the heart.

Positive personal change always begins with a desire to be different, often motivated by pain. Ideally, we then acknowledge our need for help. Like the tax collector in Luke (and the centurion in Matthew 8), each of us must accept that "I deserve nothing," that "the good things God provides are sheer gifts—I did not earn them and I could not earn them if it were up to me." Those of us who are not economically poor can be fooled into thinking we are in control, that we can handle whatever happens. We can lose our sense of spiritual poverty, the recognition that we must depend on God for our very survival.

Jesus stated, "I am the vine; you are the branches. If a man remains in me and I in him, he will bear much fruit; apart from me you can do nothing" (John 15:5). The question, though, is whether our acceptance of these ideas is mere mental agreement or true heartfelt conviction.

The Problem with Pride

The problem with pride is that the more we think we have repented of it, the more prideful we may be. Several years ago I saw a book called *The Prideful Soul's Guide to Humility.*[1] When I purchased it I was struck by a strange paradox: I felt proud to be buying it because that meant I was humble enough to admit I needed it. But feeling proud about my humility only made me more prideful! This just showed me that I am in constant need of God's grace and mercy. It also took me back to this first beatitude: I really am poor in spirit—spiritually bankrupt—in my own power.

The times I have fallen on my face and been totally humiliated have resulted from puffing myself up and acting independently, as if I did not need God's help or the help of anyone else.

Several years ago I was directing the children's ministry of a large San Francisco church. Someone I did not know called to request help for a "good cause." Without seeking advice, I sent out a group e-mail to our entire ministry staff and leadership team, "preaching" to them about the biblical mandate for this kind of benevolent work and challenging them to "get on the bandwagon."

The following day, I learned that this particular cause was not so worthy after all—and I had to send a retraction, along with an apology for my out-of-control pride and independence.

Pride is a sin that we can tend to take lightly. We feel disgust at sexual sins, but to God, pride is probably more vile than these other sins we find so shocking. Consider that pride was the sin that resulted in the fall of man:

> The woman said to the serpent, "We may eat fruit from the trees in the garden, but God did say, 'You must not eat fruit from the tree that is in the middle of the garden, and you must not touch it, or you will die.'"
>
> "You will not surely die," the serpent said to the woman. "For God

> knows that when you eat of it your eyes will be opened, and you will be like God, knowing good and evil." (Genesis 3:2–5)

The desire to "be like God" involves pride and idolatry—making ourselves gods by believing that we can manage life without his help. This passage also illustrates how pride is the root of disobedience, which resulted when Adam and Eve chose to trust and follow their own judgment rather than God's.

Another familiar example in the Bible is the story of Saul and David. God punished Saul for his pride and disobedience by rejecting him as king (1 Samuel 15:1–31). When given opportunities to repent of his pride, Saul only dug a deeper hole of sin. For example, he sounded humble and contrite for trying to murder David (1 Samuel 24:1–22), but then not long afterwards, he was after David again, and trying to hold on to his position as king rather than surrendering to God's will (1 Samuel 26:1–2).

The man chosen to replace him was David, who ended up committing adultery and murder. How was it that David ended up being called "a man after God's own heart" (1 Samuel 13:14)? When Nathan confronted David on these grievous sins, David humbled himself (2 Samuel 12:13, Psalm 51). As a result, he continued to walk with God throughout his life.

The Power of Humility

Paul taught about this kind of humility. He writes to the Romans:"Do not think of yourself more highly than you ought, but rather think of yourself with sober judgment" (Romans 12:3b).

A few years later he calls the Philippians to imitate the humility of Christ:

> Your attitude should be the same as that of Christ Jesus:
>
> Who, being in very nature God,

> did not consider equality with God something to be grasped. (Philippians 2:5–6)

Now you may be thinking, "I already feel bad about myself. Won't humbling myself make me feel even worse?" This is a valid concern, considering the epidemic of people feeling worthless and unable to reach some imaginary bar.[2] It seems that the more motivational speakers tell us we can do anything we decide to do, the more we feel guilty because we do not measure up. In other words, the higher our expectations, the more we are likely to experience disappointment.

Not surprisingly, the Bible contains the solution to this dilemma: *we are to esteem God and rely on him to help us achieve good things.* Although God loves and values us even in our sin, we can only reach our true potential and worth when we follow and obey him:

> But they would not listen and were as stiff-necked as their fathers, who did not trust in the LORD their God. They rejected his decrees and the covenant he had made with their fathers and the warnings he had given them. They followed worthless idols and themselves became worthless. (2 Kings 17:14–15)

Jesus comforted his disciples with the promise, "I tell you the truth, anyone who has faith in me will do what I have been doing. He will do even greater things than these, because I am going to the Father" (John 14:12). Here, he was referring to the empowerment of the Holy Spirit, not that they could do great things on their own.

The Scriptures make it clear that the self-confident will be insecure, while the God-confident will be secure. Reflect on the following verses:

> Hezekiah trusted in the LORD, the God of Israel. There was no one like him among all the kings of Judah, either before him or after him. He held fast to the LORD and did not cease to follow him; he kept the com-

> mands the LORD had given Moses. And the LORD was with him; he was successful in whatever he undertook. (2 Kings 18:5–7)

> He who trusts in himself is a fool,
> but he who walks in wisdom is kept safe. (Proverbs 28:26)

> See, I lay a stone in Zion, a chosen and precious cornerstone [Jesus], and the one who trusts in him will never be put to shame. (1 Peter 2:6)

Now consider the fate of those who rely on themselves:

> They will flee to caverns in the rocks and to the overhanging crags from dread of the LORD and the splendor of his majesty, when he rises to shake the earth. Stop trusting in man, who has but a breath in his nostrils. Of what account is he? (Isaiah 2:21–22)

> Woe to those who go down to Egypt for help, who rely on horses, who trust in the multitude of their chariots and in the great strength of their horsemen, but do not look to the Holy One of Israel, or seek help from the LORD. (Isaiah 31:1)

The more we rely on God's love and his word to know our own worth, the more we will be able to see ourselves as God sees us—precious and honored in his sight (Isaiah 43:4), salt of the earth and light of the world (Matthew 5:13–14), saints (Romans 1:7), the righteousness of God (2 Corinthians 5:21), strong in his mighty power (Ephesians 6:10), chosen by God (Colossians 3:12) and able to be confident on the day of judgment (1 John 4:17).

For More Reflection

1. What kinds of "worthwhile things" would you do if you were assured of God's help?
2. As you read Luke 18:9–14, who do you most identify with—the Pharisee or the tax collector? Why?

3. How self-reliant are you? Do you seek advice when faced with decisions, or do you operate independently, preferring to be the "captain of your own ship"?

4. On a scale of one to ten, how is your self-worth? Is your sense of worth based on your achievements or on God's perspective of who you are?

Step 2:
Be Desperate

"You say, 'I am rich; I have acquired wealth and do not need a thing.' But you do not realize that you are wretched, pitiful, poor, blind and naked. I counsel you to buy from me gold refined in the fire, so you can become rich; and white clothes to wear, so you can cover your shameful nakedness; and salve to put on your eyes, so you can see." (Revelation 3:17–18)

I recently participated in a women's small-group discussion. We talked about the chapter called "Am I Enough?" from Robin Weidner's book, *Secure in Heart*.[3] I was surprised to discover that every one of those intelligent, talented Christian women tended to live lives ruled by fear.

What prevents us from saying—and living as if we believe—that "I can do everything through him who gives me strength" (Philippians 4:13)? This is a question I have asked God many times—since I am one of those women! I think the answer is that most of the time I have been content to live an ordinary life, relying on my own skills and experiences, so that only occasionally have I been driven to call out for God's help.

But in those times that I make up my mind to live out his *extra*ordinary plan for my life, I'm able to see that, without relying on God, I'm really incapable of living in a way that pleases him and results in the kind of blessing he wants to provide. Then, I get desperate for God's help.

In Psalm 79:8, Asaph prays, "May your mercy come quickly to meet us, for we are in desperate need." This is exactly where Jesus wants us. Several times in my life when I was at the end of my rope, when I became really desperate for God to intervene, I have experienced "minor miracles."

One desperate situation occurred when I found out unexpectedly that I had to do a public presentation in order to get a contract for some training work. I only had five minutes to prepare. Heart pounding, I prayed, "God, I have no idea what I'm going to say, so I'm counting on you to take over if you want me to get this work."

Afterwards I had no memory of what I said during the presentation, but friends in the audience were amazed at how articulate and confident I seemed. And we got the contract!

On another occasion, several years before I was baptized into Christ, I had been trying to stop smoking for months and finally admitted to myself and to God that I was addicted and could not stop on my own. Desperately, I prayed that God would do "whatever it took" to take this awful habit away from me.

The following morning I awoke with a sore throat. Assuming I was getting a cold, I avoided smoking for a few days until I felt better. Then I tried smoking again, but as soon as I would put a cigarette in my mouth, I would get an instant sore throat. This lasted six months (and I was not sick). I could say I stopped smoking, but actually God did it—I just cooperated. Thinking back, I know that God was encouraging me to keep believing and seeking him, even during those years in my "spiritual desert."

Rely on God

As the writer of Hebrews reminds us, we should not hesitate to call on God:

> For we do not have a high priest who is unable to sympathize with our

> weaknesses, but we have one who has been tempted in every way, just as we are—yet was without sin. Let us then approach the throne of grace with confidence, so that we may receive mercy and find grace to help us in our time of need. (Hebrews 4:15–16)

In fact, God will keep challenging us until we are forced to depend on him. Paul writes:

> We do not want you to be uninformed, brothers, about the hardships we suffered in the province of Asia. We were under great pressure, far beyond our ability to endure, so that we despaired even of life. Indeed, in our hearts we felt the sentence of death. But this happened that we might not rely on ourselves but on God, who raises the dead. (2 Corinthians 1:8–9)

Our lives would be so much easier if we did not wait until we were desperate, but expected and trusted him to strengthen and help us through each day (Psalm 5:3).

God intends that sin—whether by us or against us—will drive us to rely on God. In *The Victory of Surrender,* Gordon Ferguson says, "He is lovingly trying to break us in order that he might really bless us."[4] In our culture of quick-fix coping skills and pills to alleviate discomfort, though, we may never get desperate enough to experience the kind of healing that only the great Comforter can provide (2 Corinthians 1:3–4).

Unfortunately, some people allow suffering to drive them away from God, choosing to believe Satan's lie that their suffering is a sign that God could not possibly love them. "Clara" was molested over a period of ten years.

Although she had cried out to God during these times, she believed that he never heard or answered her. Despite really wanting and needing God's healing, tragically she was unable to accept that he is a loving, compassionate Father who will never abandon us, no matter what happens.

Benefits of Suffering

We must remember that "faith is being sure of what we hope for and certain of what we do not see" (Hebrews 11:1), and that while God uses everything to bless us, we become more like Jesus as we go through suffering (Romans 8:28–29).

Because I have heard so many people use suffering as a reason for not believing in a compassionate God, several years ago I did a Bible study on why God allows suffering. Notice that each of the following involves a blessing from God.

- We learn obedience (Hebrews 5:8, Psalm 119:71).
- We learn to rely on God (2 Corinthians 1:8–9).
- We learn that there are negative consequences to sin (Genesis 4:6–12).
- God is working to change our lives (2 Corinthians 7:9–11).
- Our faith is being tested so it will be strengthened (1 Peter 1:7).
- We are being prepared to help others going through the same difficulties (2 Corinthians 1:3–5).
- We gain strength and depth (1 Peter 4:1–2).
- We develop perseverance and maturity (James 1:2–5).
- God is helping us avoid a life of evil (Job 36:21).
- Our endurance increases (Romans 5:3).
- We experience fellowship with Christ (Philippians 3:10).

How different these are from the messages sent by our humanistic society. A Grammy-winning song states, "Learning to love yourself is the greatest love of all." Motivational speakers tell us, "If you can believe it, you can achieve it." We are encouraged to believe in ourselves, build ourselves up, become more self-reliant and avoid suffering at all costs.

As disciples of Jesus, we must guard against the temptation to believe these platitudes. Our beliefs may seem strange to some. This is why Paul reminds us that "the message of the cross is foolishness to those who are perishing." But to us as Christians, "it is the power of God" (1 Corinthians 1:18).

For More Reflection

1. Think of a time when you were desperate for God's help. What did you do? What happened?

2. In what areas do you need God right now?

3. When faced with great pressure or stress, do you stop to pray, or do you become more self-reliant, making plans and to-do lists? Are you aware at these times that God is encouraging you to rely on him?

Step 3:
Be Eager

> And without faith it is impossible to please God, because anyone who comes to him must believe that he exists and that he rewards those who earnestly seek him. (Hebrews 11:6)

Throughout the Bible, God consistently implores us to seek a relationship with him. But what does it really mean to seek God? In the Old Testament, two different Hebrew words are used for seeking: *darash* and *baqash*. *Darash* means "to seek, inquire or consult" (as in Exodus 18:15 where Moses says that the people inquire of God's will). *Baqash* means "to seek, search, look for or inquire about" (as in Psalm 40:16 where David writes, "May all who seek you rejoice and be glad in you").

In the New Testament, the Greek word *zeteo* is used, meaning "to look for, seek out, try to obtain, desire to possess, or strive for." For example, Jesus tells his followers:

> "Ask and it will be given to you; seek and you will find; knock and the

> door will be opened to you. For everyone who asks receives; he who seeks finds; and to him who knocks, the door will be opened." (Matthew 7:7–8)

Other New Testament passages use the word *ekzeteo,* which means "to seek out, seek earnestly, search intently and with the greatest care, to be held responsible" (see Acts 15:17 and Hebrews 11:6).

Seeking God

I recently met with "Darlene," a young woman who reported feeling depressed. She has recently undergone some serious illness, as well as a series of deaths and disappointments. Once full of enthusiasm, Darlene has clearly lost her zest for life. No longer trusting that God has a great plan for her future, she finds herself wondering if her life is over (although she is only in her thirties.) At one point I asked her if she is still "seeking God."

She thought for a moment and replied, "No—I guess I've lost the faith to believe he still loves me and will answer my prayers."

Despite continuing to serve and participate in church activities, Darlene has exchanged her once-vibrant zeal for a dutiful "church member" mentality. To seek God, Darlene and the rest of us will need to have the three following characteristics.

1. Have a Soft Heart

We must be willing to feel again, to make ourselves vulnerable and open to God's influence. This can be difficult if we have been betrayed, abused or hurt in some significant way. To protect ourselves from further injury, we may erect walls around our feelings, refusing to allow anyone or anything to hurt us again. The result is a hard, bitter heart, unable to feel our own pain or the pain of others.

Several years ago I was telling a friend about some traumatic events from my childhood. She expressed concern that I was able to discuss these experiences with very little emotion, almost as if they had happened to someone else. She encouraged me to give myself permission to feel again and grieve.

I spent a day sitting in a park, thinking about all I had been through and asking God to help me cry. Nothing happened. Two days later was Sunday, and from the moment I arrived at church I was an emotional basket case! By the time the service ended, I had used most of a box of tissues. God answered my prayer, but not in the way I expected. Although I felt embarrassed by all my tears, he must have known I needed the comfort of caring, spiritual friends to get through the pain.

Since that time, I have not only been more able to experience my own feelings but also more able to respond to others with empathy and compassion. Hosea writes:

> Sow for yourselves righteousness,
>   reap the fruit of unfailing love,
> and break up your unplowed ground;
>   for it is time to seek the Lord,
> until he comes
>   and showers righteousness on you. (Hosea 10:12)

Just as unplowed ground is too hard for sowing seed, an "unplowed" heart prevents us from sowing the righteousness needed for earnestly seeking God. Allowing ourselves to be vulnerable requires that we humble ourselves and face our own weakness.

2. Seek God Wholeheartedly

Moses tells the Israelites, "But if from there you seek the LORD your God, you will find him if you look for him with all your heart and with all your soul" (Deuteronomy 4:29).

Through Jeremiah, God promises: "You will seek me and find me when you seek me with all your heart" (Jeremiah 29:13).

The Bible makes it clear that we can know God, and that he wants to be known—but we must sincerely want to know him. God responds to those who are passionately committed to finding him, not to those who mindlessly "go through the motions" of religious rituals.

There's a big difference between casually glancing around and seeking something with all our hearts. I can remember that, growing up, my son, Greg, always thought it was easier to go to "Mom" than to look for something on his own. He would ask, "Where are the scissors?" I would tell him, but he would return again a few minutes later saying he still couldn't find them. My response would be, "Well, you must not have looked very hard!"

In contrast, my mother used a strange expression: she would say, "I wanted it so bad I could taste it!" This always made me imagine seeing a hot fudge sundae just out of reach. Or pursuing a dream which was still far in the distance but worth every bit of energy and effort to accomplish.

3. Make God First Priority

> "So do not worry, saying, 'What shall we eat?' or 'What shall we drink?' or 'What shall we wear?' For the pagans run after all these things, and your heavenly Father knows that you need them. But seek first his kingdom and his righteousness, and all these things will be given to you as well." (Matthew 6:31–33)

For many, religious life becomes just one of several roles and responsibilities, rather than the doorway through which all of life flows. Since God is sovereign and in control, when we put him first, there is no need for worry or anxiety. Surely this was the secret to Paul's joy in the midst of trial:

> I know what it is to be in need, and I know what it is to have plenty. I have learned the secret of being content in any and every situation,

> whether well fed or hungry, whether living in plenty or in want. I can do everything through him who gives me strength. (Philippians 4:12–13)

On a practical level, how can we make God our first priority when every day is already full of pressure and responsibility? When we are juggling multiple roles (parent, spouse, employee, student, neighbor, daughter, sister, etc.), the days seem to fly by with no opportunity to think, let alone pray or reflect on Scripture. Here are a few suggestions for growing spiritually in spite of a packed schedule:

- Take opportunities to pray throughout the day—while driving, showering, folding laundry.
- Have a short daily devotional with your children—reading or acting out a favorite Bible story, and praying together for God's help with difficult situations.
- Talk with your children about God and, as they get older, share scriptures with them to help them face challenges with peers or at school.
- Each morning, set your alarm to get up at least a half hour earlier for a personal "quiet time" with God, and let family members know how important this is to you so they will be less likely to interrupt you. Take your Bible to work and read it during your lunch break.
- Write encouraging scriptures on note cards or Post-it notes and put them on your mirror, refrigerator, bulletin board or desk.
- For one week, keep a detailed record of how you spend your time. Look for opportunities to spend extra time with God by cutting out some TV time or limiting the length of phone calls.
- Find a friend from church who also wants to grow spiritually. Get together once a week to pray together and share challenges and Bible solutions.
- Invite a group of coworkers to meet once a week at lunch to study and discuss an inspiring Bible-based book.

For More Reflection

1. Are you "stuck" in your current relationship with God, or are you continuing to seek him with all your heart? Why do you think our joy level rises as we commit to seek him with all our heart?

2. Are you willing to be vulnerable and open to influence by God's word or Christian friends, even if it means seeing unpleasant things about yourself?

3. Does your inner peace in the face of pressure reveal your trust in God, or do you feel controlled by worry and stress?

4. Are you taking the risks necessary to be desperate for God's help?

5. What's your first priority? Do you spend daily time in prayer and Bible study? Do you rely on God throughout each day?

❄

Our reward for humbly seeing our need, recognizing our desperate circumstances and eagerly seeking his favor is simple—God gives us his kingdom! In essence, God "moves in"—he takes up residence in our hearts. He guides us and exercises his benevolent control in our lives. He reigns over us, merging our will with his, giving us a hunger to know him more intimately, walk with him and honor him in everything.

James puts it this way: "Humble yourselves before the Lord, and he will lift you up in honor." (James 4:10, NLT)

3

Contrition

Imagine God's Comfort

"Blessed are those who mourn,
for they will be comforted."
Matthew 5:4

At first glance, it seems obvious that, since God is the great Comforter (Jeremiah 8:18), he will comfort us when we are mourning over the loss of a loved one. But when we consider Jesus' statement in the context of the other beatitudes, it becomes clear that Jesus is talking about a very specific type of mourning—mourning over our spiritual poverty, our sin. What could this kind of mourning possibly have to do with discovering inner joy?

Adam Clarke's old English commentary reads a bit awkwardly to us in this century, but his wisdom still comes through:

> Every one flies from sorrow, and seeks after joy, and yet true joy must necessarily be the fruit of sorrow. The whole need not (do not feel the need of) the physician, but they that are sick do; i.e., they who are sensible of their disease. Only such persons as are deeply convinced of the sinfulness of sin, feel the plague of their own heart, and turn with disgust from all worldly consolations, because of their insufficiency to render them happy, have God's promise of solid comfort.[1]

Matthew Henry puts it this way, "Heaven is the joy of our Lord; a mountain of joy, to which our way is through a vale of tears."[2] We must willingly suffer pain in order to achieve great joy. Childbirth is my favorite analogy. If I had been unwilling to face the pain of labor and delivery, God would never have been able to bless me with the amazing experience of motherhood.

But the question is, "If being conscious of our sinfulness is so important, why do many people rarely speak of sin?" I recall posing this question to a ministry friend some years ago. Her response was that many people consider discussions about sin discouraging, and churches may not want to discourage their congregations, particularly when their membership is already dwindling.

Sadly, this comment reveals how even well-meaning Christians can fall prey to a desire to "please the people," and as a result end up following humanistic leaders who believe that flattery is the way to protect our fragile self-worth.

Another reason we do not continue to deal with our sin is our mistaken belief that if we are truly disciples of Jesus, we will no longer give in to sin. We deceive ourselves and think we have no sin.

Although the Holy Spirit empowers us, it is still clear that "if we claim to be without sin, we deceive ourselves and the truth is not in us" (1 John 1:8). God wants us to have an awareness of our sin, which leads to a "contrite" (crushed) heart. This he ultimately rewards with his presence and his comfort:

> For this is what the high and lofty One says—
> he who lives forever, whose name is holy:
> "I live in a high and holy place,
> but also with him who is contrite and lowly in spirit,
> to revive the spirit of the lowly and
> to revive the heart of the contrite." (Isaiah 57:15)

Now close your eyes and...

Imagine God's Comfort

Isn't it incredible to realize that the Creator of the universe wants a personal relationship with each of us? In Matthew 23, Jesus minces no words in rebuking the hypocrisy of the Pharisees. The striking thing about this passage, though, is that just a few verses after calling them a brood of vipers who may not escape hell (v33), he goes on to say,

> "How often I have longed to gather your children together, as a hen gathers her chicks under her wings, but you were not willing." (v37)

He wants to comfort and revive us whenever we are discouraged or beaten down by life's pressures. As the perfect Father, his love and his availability are unconditional—not dependent on our perfection. For many of us, it is difficult to imagine a Father like that, since our view of God is limited by experience with our earthly fathers (who are as imperfect as we are).

Because Jesus paid the price for our sin on the cross (Romans 5:8), God expects us to fully acknowledge and feel the impact of who we are. This then motivates us to continually repent and rely even more on his help. In other words, we need to

- Get Vulnerable: Recognize and acknowledge our sin.
- Get Real: Identify specific sins and grieve over how they hurt God and other people.
- Get Going: Take action to repent.

First, let's look at what it means in our lives when we decide to get humble and to see our sin as God sees it—and to stop deceiving ourselves and rationalizing it away.

Step 1: Get Vulnerable

> Come and listen, all you who fear God;
> let me tell you what he has done for me.
> I cried out to him with my mouth;
> his praise was on my tongue.

If I had cherished sin in my heart,
  the LORD would not have listened;
but God has surely listened
  and heard my voice in prayer. (Psalm 66:16–19)

If it were up to me, I would usually choose the most comfortable path. Because of my basic insecurity, I hate facing my flaws and instead prefer to think I am "good enough." For many years I looked at my life this way, comparing myself to other people whose sins seemed to be a lot worse than mine. I figured that God must be pretty happy with me since I was not out murdering anyone or robbing banks.

Perhaps because of my ignorance, God was merciful with me. But then I learned what the Bible really says, and I was forced to face the facts about myself. I have found that there are many reasons we deceive ourselves.

1. Modern-Day Idolatry

Idolatry is one reason we deceive ourselves. Although we may not actually bow down to wooden statues, when we love the things of this life more than God and his word, we are guilty of idolatry:

He feeds on ashes, a deluded heart misleads him;
he cannot save himself, or say,
"Is not this thing in my right hand a lie?" (Isaiah 44:20)

How would idolatry lead us into self-deception? Our desire for and enjoyment of pleasure can blind us, making us unwilling to make the sacrifices necessary to really put God first.

When Jesus says, "In the same way, any of you who does not give up everything he has cannot be my disciple" (Luke 14:33), he means that if we truly love God with all our heart, soul and mind (Matthew 22:37), we should be eager to do whatever it takes to serve God and other people.

As we watch Jesus, we see that for each individual the need will be different. Perhaps Jesus knew that the woman at the well was thirsting for contentment in all her marriages, so he talked to her about "living water" (John 4:4–26). On the other hand, he knew that money was the rich young man's god, so he said,

> "Sell your possessions and give to the poor, and you will have treasure in heaven. Then, come follow me." (Matthew 19:21)

But when he called Zacchaeus, the tax collector, he said, "Zacchaeus…I must stay at your house today," knowing that once Zacchaeus came to know him personally, he would repent of his greed quickly—and that he would decide on his own to give half of his possessions to the poor and make restitution to those he had cheated (Luke 19:1–9).

I believe that we all struggle with some form of idolatry, someone or something that we put before God. Can you identify your idol? It may be your spouse, children, good health, friends. It may be an addiction to work, food or alcohol. Or it may be more abstract, like your reputation, career, comfort or appearance.

Perfection: For "Felicia," perfection is an idol. Diagnosed with a rare medical condition as a preteen, she struggled with the painful belief that she was a "freak of nature." Rather than helping her share her intense humiliation and feelings of rejection, in their own sadness and disappointment her parents told her to "just be strong." As a result, she learned to pretend. Felicia excelled academically throughout high school and college and, blessed with a beautiful singing voice, she won various awards in vocal competitions.

No one guessed how unhappy and inadequate she felt, so other young women thought Felicia would never understand their struggles, and she missed out on the peer friendship, support and fun that is so important during adolescence and early adulthood. Only now, as a young adult, she is confronting the deeply buried sense of worthlessness that has paralyzed her and stunted her emotional and spiritual growth.

Ask Ourselves: We need to ask ourselves what idols we might have. Sometimes I ask myself what I would do if my husband and son fell away from God. Would I still be faithful? What if they not only lost their faith but no longer approved of my devotion to the gospel? I know that this would be a huge challenge, especially since I am aware that their acceptance is very important—maybe even an idol—for me. But Jesus says I must love him more than anyone else (Luke 14:26). I want to have a gentle and quiet spirit so that whatever happens, I can put my hope in God and not give way to fear (1 Peter 3:4–6).

Sometimes our idols are revealed by the ways we struggle with certain sins. I have struggled with sharing my faith—talking about what God has done and encouraging others to seek a relationship with him. This is especially difficult when I am around "important people"—other psychologists, community leaders, high-powered businesswomen. In these situations my fear of rejection is so intense that, even when I do speak up, I am timid and fearful instead of bold and confident.

Just as I want the acceptance of my family, approval of these leaders is an idol for me, which certainly does not please God. Although I have tried a variety of things—thinking about the worst thing that could happen, analyzing the childhood root of my fear, and looking at scriptures about the importance of pleasing God instead of people—I still have not been able to completely overcome my cowardice.

Lately I have been thinking that the answer lies in relying on God more, stepping out in faith in spite of my fear, so that his power can be made perfect in my weakness (2 Corinthians 12:9). I will continue working on this aspect of my character for as long as it takes.

Feeling in Control: For many of us, feeling in control can be an idol. When we feel out of control or sense that our control is slipping, we exert an extreme effort to control the other people in our lives. Not only are we guilty of idolatry, we are actually harming them as well. Of course we think what we are doing is "for their own good," but rather than being patient for God to work, we try to "help out" and end up trying to take his place.

This may reflect a problem called codependence. It involves a cycle of control, manipulation, enabling and rescuing that ultimately prevents others from experiencing the consequences of their actions. According to the authors of *Some Sat in Darkness: Spiritual Recovery from Addiction and Codependency,*

> God sees codependency as a specific group of sins linked together which prevent people from going to heaven. It is far more serious than a behavioral addiction. At the very core, codependency is a lack of trust in God and reveals a heart that has not surrendered. It is sin and it is deadly.[3]

They go on to explain that God intends the consequences of our decisions to make us see our need for him, but when we control people and "protect" them from experiencing pain, we are really standing in the way of God's plan.

Examples from Scripture: A need to feel in control can be a significant challenge for those who suffer from psychological disorders that rob them of the ability to control their own emotional reactions. Although medications can sometimes be helpful, this can also be an opportunity to learn to trust and rely on a God who understands emotional pain. Scripture abounds with models to encourage and teach us: the heroes of the faith may have accomplished great things for God, but that does not mean they did not suffer in the same ways we do.

We usually remember Job for the way he valiantly resisted the sin of blaming God (Job 1:20–22), but if we keep reading, we discover that he eventually plummeted into depression (Job 10:1–19). These verses indicate that he hated his life, he imagined that God was angry with him, he felt guilty and worthless, and he even developed what mental health people call "passive-suicidal thinking" (vv18–19).

David also experienced depression (Psalms 6, 13 and 38), as did Elijah (1 Kings 19:4).

Moses, Gideon and Paul suffered a lack of confidence (Exodus 4–6, Judges 6:11–40, 1 Corinthians 2:3).

Jesus suffered such distress that his sweat fell like drops of blood (Luke 22:44). Although he never sinned, he was tempted to forsake the cross when he considered what was ahead, and perhaps even struggled not to be angry when his closest friends could not even stay awake during his hour of greatest need (Matthew 26:36–46).

2. Feel Good About Ourselves

A second reason we deceive ourselves about our sin is a need to feel good about ourselves. In order to pump up our self-esteem, we flatter ourselves:

> An oracle is within my heart
> concerning the sinfulness of the wicked:
> There is no fear of God
> before his eyes.
> For in his own eyes he flatters himself
> too much to detect or hate his sin. (Psalm 36:1–2)

Or, like the Pharisee in Luke 18:10–14, we may sincerely believe we are righteous. To this person, Paul says: "If anyone thinks he is something when he is nothing, he deceives himself. Each one should test his own actions" (Galatians 6:3–4).

If seeing our own sin is so painful, why is it necessary? Because God hates sin. To appreciate how strongly he feels, look at the language Jesus uses in the following passage:

> "But if anyone causes one of these little ones who believe in me to sin, it would be better for him to have a large millstone hung around his neck and to be drowned in the depths of the sea.
>
> "Woe to the world because of the things that cause people to sin! Such things must come, but woe to the man through whom they come! If your hand or your foot causes you to sin, cut it off and throw it away. It is better for you to enter life maimed or crippled than to have two hands or two feet and be thrown into eternal fire. And if your eye causes you to sin, gouge it out and throw it away. It is better for you to enter life with one eye than to have two eyes and be thrown into the fire of hell." (Matthew 18:6–9)

Since our repentance rests on recognizing the ways we are disobedient, *seeing our sin* is the first step toward getting right with God.

Second, *being grateful for God's forgiveness* is directly related to accurately seeing our spiritual condition, and the fact that we do not deserve anything but eternal damnation. From a worldly perspective this statement may seem harsh in a book devoted to discovering joy, but nevertheless it is true, and, as we will see, it does bring us to joy.

Finally, *acknowledging our sin* keeps us humble, which is essential in our relationship with God and with other people. James advises, "Confess your sins to each other and pray for each other so that you may be healed" (James 5:16). We are much more likely to be gracious with others when we admit how much we need compassion and grace ourselves.

For More Reflection

1. To determine in what areas you may be tempted with idolatry, pray through the following questions:
    - What am I not willing to give up or do for Jesus?
    - On what is my security based?
    - What kind of loss would make me question or even fall away from God?

2. What happens when you feel out-of-control? Do you try to control or rescue people around you? Or are you willing to let God work in their lives by allowing them to feel the consequences of their decisions?

3. How do you handle emotional pain? Do you go to the Bible for encouragement, hope, joy and help, or do you allow Satan to use discouragement to drive you away from God?

4. Are you willing to work on recognizing and acknowledging your sin, even though it may be temporarily painful? Do you trust that God will turn your wailing into dancing and clothe you with joy (Psalm 30:11)?

Step 2: Get Real

> Submit yourselves, then, to God. Resist the devil, and he will flee from you. Come near to God and he will come near to you. Wash your hands, you sinners, and purify your hearts, you double-minded. Grieve, mourn and wail. Change your laughter to mourning and your joy to gloom. Humble yourselves before the Lord, and he will lift you up. (James 4:7–10)

The next step after getting vulnerable is to identify our specific sins. But how can we do this if we are so adept at deceiving ourselves? A good place to begin is in *prayer*, asking God to reveal anything that displeases him. Consider the prayer of David:

> Search me, O God, and know my heart;
>   test me and know my anxious thoughts.
> See if there is any offensive way in me,
>   and lead me in the way everlasting. (Psalm 139:23–24)

Praying through some of the lists of sin found in Scripture is also useful. The following passages will get you started:

- Matthew 15:19–20
- Romans 1:29–32
- 1 Corinthians 6:9–10
- Galatians 5:19–21
- Ephesians 4:17–5:14
- Colossians 3:5–9
- 2 Timothy 3:1–5
- James 4:17
- Revelation 21:8

Several years ago during a worship service the preacher suggested that we *study the Gospels,* keeping a chart with three columns: (1) scripture reference (chapter and verse); (2) what Jesus said or did; (3) what I would usually say or do. I started studying Matthew, and was shocked at all the ways I don't respond as Jesus did. I realized I had a lot to work on.

Finally, *ask your spouse or a trusted Christian friend* to point out the ways they believe you can grow to be more like Jesus and, if possible, show you a scripture to back up their comments. For example, if they notice that you easily become impatient with your daughter, they might remind you that love is patient (1 Corinthians 13:4). This kind of feedback can be difficult to hear, since it involves asking for correction, but your eagerness to grow spiritually can also inspire your spouse or friend to do the same, resulting in a partnership in which you can help one another.

Despite the fact that people often seek professional help when faced with personal or interpersonal challenges, as a psychologist I have often reflected that when we use the Scriptures to help each other as God intended, this spiritual feedback can help us remain emotionally and spiritually healthy, reducing the need for professional counseling.

In *Discipling: God's Plan to Train and Transform His People*, author

Gordon Ferguson argues that in all our relationships in the body of Christ (the church), we are to work together to help each other be faithful disciples of Jesus.[4] Ferguson lists fifty-six "one-another passages" that are mentioned in the New Testament (NIV translation). We are told to love one another (John 13:34–35); encourage one another daily (Hebrews 3:13); spur one another on toward love and good deeds (Hebrews 10:24); submit to one another (Ephesians 5:21); instruct one another (Romans 15:14); be devoted to one another (Romans 12:10); serve one another (Galatians 5:13); speak to one another with psalms, hymns and spiritual songs (Ephesians 5:19); teach and admonish one another (Colossians 3:16); build each other up (I Thessalonians 5:11); and clothe ourselves with humility toward one another (1 Peter 5:5). Obviously, God expects us to help each other enjoy the full life he offers and make it to heaven.[5]

Humility in Relationships

Although there have been many times in my life that I learned—often the hard way —the importance of humility in relationships, an example that stands out is my struggle to be close to another woman leader in our church. Although for a time we fooled many into thinking we were best friends, in truth we had developed deep resentment and bitterness toward each other. We both felt painfully impotent and hopeless about the possibility of change, although we knew our relationship wasn't pleasing or glorifying to God.

Each time other leaders would counsel us about the importance of unity we would make an all-out effort to change, but the improvement would be temporary, so that a month later we would be back to where we began. Because we were trying to change our behavior without changing our hearts, it isn't surprising that we were unsuccessful.

Fortunately, both of us were pleading with God to intervene, and he did! During a church conference, a former ministry leader volunteered to act as our mediator. My heart broke as I listened to my friend share all that she had experienced in our relationship. I had to face the fact that I am not naturally considerate and thoughtful. And, although my training has taught me some *skills* for building relationships, without a heart full of love these skills are of little value.

The great news is that since then we have both had a change of *heart* (followed by a change of behavior), so that we are closer now than we ever thought possible. God has miraculously healed us; for the first time we truthfully can say we are best friends.

Grieve over Sin

Once we are able to see our sin, God wants us to feel its impact, to grieve and understand, at a heart level, the pain it causes:

> Because your heart was responsive and you humbled yourself before the LORD when you heard what I have spoken against this place and its people, that they would become accursed and laid waste, and because you tore your robes and wept in my presence, I have heard you, declares the LORD. (2 Kings 22:19)

In our worldliness we tend to minimize the consequences of sin. Most of us recognize that sin *angers* God, but the fact is that our sin also *hurts* God. Before the flood, God looked at the world and was saddened by what had become of his perfect creation:

> Now the LORD observed the extent of the people's wickedness, and he saw that all their thoughts were consistently and totally evil. So the LORD was sorry he had ever made them. It broke his heart. (Genesis 6:5–6, NLT)

The fact that God is so adamant about our repentance is actually evidence of his love. Consider just a few of the ways that our sin harms us:

- It masters us (Genesis 4:7).
- It causes us to speak evil (Job 15:5).
- It causes us to waste away (Psalm 106:43).
- It rules over us (Psalm 119:133).
- It holds us fast (Proverbs 5:22).
- It disgraces us (Proverbs 14:34).
- It ensnares us (Proverbs 29:6).
- It causes our lives to collapse (Isaiah 30:13).
- It brings condemnation (Romans 5:16).
- It enslaves us (Romans 6:16).

Consequence of Sin

The most obvious consequence of our sin occurs in our interpersonal relationships. When we are unloving, impatient, angry, critical, unkind, harsh or unforgiving, our sin not only prevents us from living peacefully with others, it can do long-term and even eternal damage to the people in our lives. Jesus rebuked the Pharisees for being a stumbling block to people trying to enter his kingdom:

> "Woe to you, teachers of the law and Pharisees, you hypocrites! You shut the kingdom of heaven in men's faces. You yourselves do not enter, nor will you let those enter who are trying to." (Matthew 23:13)

Paul cautioned the believers against being a stumbling block to their "weaker" brothers (Romans 14:1–2, 13), and warned about being influenced by the sins of others (Galatians 6:1).

Godly Sorrow

Although our sin should cause us grief, the way we respond to this sorrow is also important. In his first letter to the Corinthians, Paul rebukes the church for their disunity and immorality, and in his second letter he acknowledges that he regretted having caused them pain. However, he goes on to say that now he is happy because their sorrow led them to repent. He then distinguishes between godly sorrow and worldly sorrow:

> Godly sorrow brings repentance that leads to salvation and leaves no regret, but worldly sorrow brings death. See what this godly sorrow has produced in you: what earnestness, what eagerness to clear yourselves, what indignation, what alarm, what longing, what concern, what readiness to see justice done. (2 Corinthians 7:10–11)

In other words, God does not want us to suffer because he is uncaring, but because he knows that this suffering will motivate a change of heart and behavior, which will ultimately be for our benefit.

Unfortunately, when it comes to sin, many of us go to one of two extremes: we either fail to acknowledge our sin (as we have already discussed), or we see it so clearly we are overwhelmed by self-pity. When Paul says that, "worldly sorrow brings death," he is talking about this kind of self-pitying "poor me" mentality—the tendency to get down on ourselves without the motivation to repent.

There have been times when I was convicted by a challenging lesson and, with great intentions, promised God I would be different from that point forward. But soon afterward, I would find myself doing the same thing I had done before making that commitment!

This is a perfect example of self-pity or worldly sorrow, since I felt guilty but still didn't choose to change. Why does worldly sorrow bring death? Because there is no heart change that leads to repentance. As a result, we continue down a slippery slope, further and further away from God.

We must realize that sin is serious business. In order to enjoy the fullness of God's blessings we need a regular "heart and life check-up," followed by appropriate acts of repentance.

For More Reflection

1. As you prayed through the lists of sins on page 56, what specif-

ic sins did you discover? If you have not yet made a list of sins you see in your life, take time to do this now.

2. For each sin you listed, write down how that sin hurts God, yourself and other people.

3. For sins that seem to be a central part of your character (those you struggle with in many different situations), write as many related scriptures as possible on note cards. Work on memorizing these verses to use as your "Sword of the Spirit" when temptation strikes (Ephesians 6:17).

4. As you study the Gospels, in what ways are you different from Jesus? Share these with a friend, and pair up to help and encourage each other become more like Jesus.

Step 3: Get Going

"When they sin against you—for there is no one who does not sin—and you become angry with them and give them over to the enemy, who takes them captive to his own land, far away or near; and if they have a change of heart in the land where they are held captive, and repent and plead with you in the land of their conquerors and say, 'We have sinned, we have done wrong, we have acted wickedly'; and if they turn back to you with all their heart and soul in the land of their enemies who took them captive, and pray to you toward the land you gave their fathers, toward the city you have chosen and the temple I have built for your Name; then from heaven, your dwelling place, hear their prayer and their plea, and uphold their cause. And forgive your people, who have sinned against you; forgive all the offenses they have committed against you, and cause their conquerors to show them mercy; for they are your people and your inheritance, whom you brought out of Egypt, out of that iron-smelting furnace.

"May your eyes be open to your servant's plea and to the plea of your people Israel, and may you listen to them whenever they cry out to you." (1 Kings 8:46–52)

After getting vulnerable and getting real, we need to do the obvious: get going, or move forward in our repentance and our relationship with God.

The previous passage is part of Solomon's prayer of dedication after completion of the temple around 959 BC. Earlier, Solomon begins by praising God. Then, having re-dedicated himself and the temple itself, he entreats God to continue to be merciful in response to his people's contrite, repentant hearts, and especially during their years of captivity. (This is prophetic because the Israelites would in fact be taken captive by the Babylonians around 597 BC—more than 300 years later!) What is important for us, though, is Solomon's phrase, "if they turn back to you with all their heart and soul."

This brings up the question, "What is biblical repentance, and why is it so important to God?" A few additional scriptures will help answer this question:

> Rid yourselves of all the offenses you have committed, and get a new heart and a new spirit. Why will you die, O house of Israel? (Ezekiel 18:31)

> Now there were some present at that time who told Jesus about the Galileans whose blood Pilate had mixed with their sacrifices. Jesus answered, "Do you think that these Galileans were worse sinners than all the other Galileans because they suffered this way? I tell you, no! But unless you repent, you too will all perish. Or those eighteen who died when the tower in Siloam fell on them—do you think they were more guilty than all the others living in Jerusalem? I tell you, no! But unless you repent, you too will all perish." (Luke 13:1–5)

> The Lord is not slow in keeping his promise, as some understand slowness. He is patient with you, not wanting anyone to perish, but everyone to come to repentance. (2 Peter 3:9)

These verses make it clear that, in God's mind, there are only two choices: repent or perish. Like our attitude toward sin, repentance is a subject of the utmost importance if we want to spend eternity with God. So it is critical that we answer the question, "Exactly what is involved in order to repent of my sin?" Consider the following passages:

> "So then, King Agrippa, I was not disobedient to the vision from heaven. First to those in Damascus, then to those in Jerusalem and in all Judea, and to the Gentiles also, I preached that they should repent and turn to God and prove their repentance by their deeds. That is why the Jews seized me in the temple courts and tried to kill me." (Acts 26:19–21)

> "Now turn from your sins and turn to God, so you can be cleansed of your sins. Then wonderful times of refreshment will come from the presence of the Lord, and he will send Jesus your Messiah to you again." (Acts 3:19–20, NLT)

The New Century Version renders the same passage:

> "So you must change your hearts and lives! Come back to God, and he will forgive your sins. Then the Lord will send the time of rest."

So repentance involves:

- A decision to change
- A radical turning away from sin
- A heart change involving turning to God
- Actions that show we have changed

The Heart of Repentance

Going back to 2 Corinthians 7:10–11, we see a description of the heart of repentance being acted out. We can look at these seven attitudes when we are needing to repent of a specific sin, and then test our hearts with them.

Description of Repentance	**Specific Sin: Being Critical (Romans 14:13)**
(1) Earnestness/sincerity	I really want to change my critical heart. No more excuses!
(2) Eagerness to clear myself	I will confess my sin and share my decision with my family members and closest friends so they can hold me accountable.
(3) Indignation about my sin	I do not like myself when I get critical. I hate this sin!
(4) Alarm/urgency	I must stop now. I cannot let this go on any longer.
(5) Longing to be right with God	I know this sin hurts God (James 1:26). I want to repent and return to a right relationship with God.
(6) Concern for those you have hurt	My criticism tears down my husband. I will humble myself and ask for forgiveness.
(7) Readiness to see justice done	I will give up anything or do whatever is necessary in order to change this aspect of my character.

But there is also good news when we repent! God promises that we will feel refreshed (Acts 3:19), that he will be compassionate and relent in his anger (Joel 2:13), and that he will hold us in high esteem (Isaiah 66:2). This is, in part, the comfort God provides when we are willing to acknowledge our vulnerability, love righteousness more than we love our good image of ourselves and get serious about repentance.

"Self-directed" personal change also has great therapeutic value. Although it's been said that "no one likes change—except a wet baby," most people are motivated to change when the pain of remaining the same becomes greater than the pain of changing. In fact, one major role of the professional counselor is to assist clients in understanding *why* certain changes should be considered, deciding *what* changes they need to undertake and *when*, and then *how* to go about making those changes.

As God's children, we have the perfect guidebook for personal change—written by the One who created us and who knows how our lives are designed to work!

For More Reflection

1. Have you ever changed in a significant way, causing people to ask, "What's come over you?"
2. Has your attitude been that sin is okay in moderation, or have you been radical in repenting (Matthew 5:29–30)?
3. Have you found it especially difficult to repent in certain areas of your life or character? Which ones, and how can you begin to see changes in these areas?
4. If, in repenting of major life or character sins, you have not had the seven characteristics of heart described in 2 Corinthians 7, are there issues you have yet to resolve?

❄

In this second beatitude, God promises that when we fully face the truth about ourselves and mourn the pain we cause him and other people, he will fill us with his comfort. He will relieve our pain and revive our broken hearts (Isaiah 57:15). Thus restored, encouraged and strengthened, we are ready to trust him even more, enabling us to surrender our lives fully and completely to his perfect will.

4

Meekness

Surrender to God

"Blessed are the meek,
for they will inherit the earth."
Matthew 5:5

Having faced and felt our spiritual bankruptcy, we are ready for step three: to adopt the meekness of Jesus. The word "meek" means to be humbly patient especially when provoked. Synonyms include submissive, yielding, serene, unperturbed and without belligerence or bad temper. Although meekness is often confused with weakness, a more accurate comparison is the "power under control" of a broken horse or a tamed lion.

Serenity is a quality most of us strive for, but the person who yields to others is usually regarded as a "Caspar Milquetoast," unlikely to make much of an impact or be taken seriously. How many of us pray for meekness? Personally, I am more likely to pray for boldness, envisioning myself as more of a warrior than as a humble servant in the background.

Because the word "meek" is rarely used in modern conversation, it is often replaced by "humble" or "gentle" in the Bible's New International Version. But the language of the King James Version clarifies the importance of this attribute.

First, God commands that we be meek (Zephaniah 2:3, KJV). In fact, meekness is necessary for salvation (Psalm 149:4, KJV) and for living in a way that glorifies God (1 Peter 3:4, KJV). Responding to God's word also requires meekness (James 1:21, KJV), as does effectively reaching the lost (1 Peter 3:15, KJV).

Jesus was the essence of meekness. As Isaiah prophesied:

> He was oppressed and afflicted,
> yet he did not open his mouth;
> he was led like a lamb to the slaughter,
> and as a sheep before her shearers is silent
> so he did not open his mouth. (Isaiah 53:7)

In a similar passage, Peter says, "When they hurled their insults at him, he did not retaliate; when he suffered, he made no threats" (1 Peter 2:23).

At the same time, Jesus was anything but weak. When he saw his Father's house being defiled, he made a whip and drove the merchants out. He was not intimidated by the Pharisees' age or status, but condemned their hypocrisy in no uncertain terms. He did not defend himself, but Jesus did not hesitate to use his power to defend God.

What does Jesus say about meekness?

> "Bless those who curse you, pray for those who mistreat you. If someone strikes you on one cheek, turn to him the other also. If someone takes your cloak, do not stop him from taking your tunic. Give to everyone who asks you, and if anyone takes what belongs to you, do not demand it back." (Luke 6:29–30)

These words strike us as unfair: does God really want us to give in to injustice or mistreatment? What would it take to willingly endure this kind of abuse?

I think the answer is "trust"! We would have to

- Give Credit: Trust God completely with our lives; affirm what he has done up until now, and decide to trust him for the future.
- Give Up: Turn control over to God, knowing his plan for us is absolutely perfect and that all things happen just as he decided long ago (Ephesians 1:11, NLT).

- Give Over: Be one hundred percent confident that God will protect us—that even if we experience pain and loss, he will be right there giving us the strength to survive and grow through the experience.

In short, we would need the faith to believe, as Paul did, that God really does work "for the good of those who love him" (Romans 8:28), and that when we suffer it is because God wants to bless us by helping us become more Christlike, conforming us "to the likeness of his Son" (Romans 8:29). Of course, our problem is that we do not define "blessing" the way God does. We think that when we are hurting, God is not blessing us! This is why we need to...

Surrender to God

Surrender is a major theme in the Bible, with many paying a steep price for resisting God. Adam chose to eat the forbidden fruit, and rather than freely enjoying God's creation, he had to work the ground, requiring backbreaking labor. Saul was rejected—and replaced—as king when he used his "common sense" and disobeyed the command to completely annihilate the Amalekites. Jonah refused the call to go to Nineveh and ended up in the belly of a whale.

As I thought about these men, I realized how each of them had tried to walk with God. They were not the pagans of the land who did not believe, but those who had chosen to follow God's way. And yet they suffered God's wrath because of their failure to surrender.

Now let us consider some whose examples are worthy of imitation. Only when understood in the context of Abraham's amazing trust that "God himself will provide the lamb for the burnt offering" (Genesis 22:8) can we begin to fathom his willingness to sacrifice his long-awaited son, Isaac. While it is tempting to think we could never have that kind of faith, we remember that this same Abraham failed to protect his wife, telling her to claim she was his sister (a deliberately misleading half-truth) to lessen the chance of the Egyptians killing him to have her for themselves (Genesis 12:10–20). Referring to this story, Peter applauds Sarah's meekness in the following familiar passage:

> For this is the way the holy women of the past who put their hope in God used to make themselves beautiful. They were submissive to their own husbands, like Sarah, who obeyed Abraham and called him her master. You are her daughters if you do what is right and do not give way to fear. (1 Peter 3:5–6)

As I consider these "holy women of the past," it occurs to me that Jesus might say we women have been given the blessing of submission, since the meek will inherit the earth, despite the way we usually view the scriptures commanding us to submit.

Then there is Mary the mother of Jesus. How many of us would so willingly put ourselves at serious risk by seeming to violate an unquestioned moral law? But when the angel explained that she was to bear the Son of God, she simply responded: "I am the Lord's servant...may it be to me as you have said" (Luke 1:38). What spiritual strength it must have taken for Mary to react this way. I am so inspired by her faith and humility. Isn't it amazing that the very source of Mary's ability to influence and impact us is her meekness? Considered this way, meekness becomes a more attractive quality.

Step 1:
Give Credit

> In the future, when your son asks you, "What is the meaning of the stipulations, decrees and laws the LORD our God has commanded you?" tell him: "We were slaves of Pharaoh in Egypt, but the LORD brought us out of Egypt with a mighty hand. Before our eyes the LORD sent miraculous signs and wonders—great and terrible—upon Egypt and Pharaoh and his whole household. But he brought us out from there to bring us in and give us the land that he promised on oath to

> our forefathers. The LORD commanded us to obey all these decrees and to fear the LORD our God, so that we might always prosper and be kept alive, as is the case today. And if we are careful to obey all this law before the LORD our God, as he has commanded us, that will be our righteousness." (Deuteronomy 6:20–25)

If we are to trust and rely on God, we must recognize the times he has intervened in our lives—just as God instructed the Jews in the passage above. Although our miracles may not seem as spectacular as those shown to the wandering Israelites, they are as real and as powerful.

Think of all the ways God works in your life. Think of the times you prayed desperate prayers for courage or protection—and God came through. In my life, there have literally been hundreds of times that I have begged God for help in some difficult circumstance, and the very thing I prayed for—or something even better—happened. Unfortunately, in many of these situations I tended to think of the result as more of a "coincidence" than as a miracle. I must constantly remind myself that God is always with me, providing the following:

Salvation

> Therefore he is able to save completely those who come to God through him, because he always lives to intercede for them. (Hebrews 7:25)

Protection

> "My prayer is not that you take them out of the world but that you protect them from the evil one." (John 17:15)

Rescue

> "The LORD who delivered me from the paw of the lion and the paw of the bear will deliver me from the hand of this Philistine." (1 Samuel 17:37)

Encouragement

You hear, O Lord, the desire of the afflicted;
you encourage them, and you listen to their cry. (Psalm 10:17)

Inspiration

"For who has known the mind of the Lord that he may instruct him?" But we have the mind of Christ. (1 Corinthians 2:16)

Reward

And without faith it is impossible to please God, because anyone who comes to him must believe that he exists and that he rewards those who earnestly seek him. (Hebrews 11:6)

Guidance

He guides me in paths of righteousness
for his name's sake. (Psalm 23:3)

Forgiveness

For he has rescued us from the dominion of darkness and brought us into the kingdom of the Son he loves, in whom we have redemption, the forgiveness of sins. (Colossians 1:13–14)

Healing

Go back and tell Hezekiah, the leader of my people, "This is what the Lord, the God of your father David, says: I have heard your prayer and seen your tears; I will heal you." (2 Kings 20:5)

Strength

And the God of all grace, who called you to his eternal glory in Christ, after you have suffered a little while, will himself restore you and make you strong, firm and steadfast. (1 Peter 5:10)

Courage

"Have I not commanded you? Be strong and courageous. Do not be

> terrified; do not be discouraged, for the LORD your God will be with you wherever you go." (Joshua 1:9)

Peace of mind

> Do not be anxious about anything, but in everything, by prayer and petition, with thanksgiving, present your requests to God. And the peace of God, which transcends all understanding, will guard your hearts and your minds in Christ Jesus. (Philippians 4:6–7)

Sometimes God does not act as quickly as we would like. Because we have to wait for his intervention, we assume he is not listening or even that he does not care. A year before this writing we had decided to make a move to be closer to my job and our ministry. We put our condo on the market. Six months later we had not even had a nibble, despite fervent prayers by us and the people in our lives.

There were times I prayed, "God, I thought you were interested in the details of my life. Does this matter to you? Can't you hear our prayers?"

Eventually we humbled out and lowered the selling price of our condo; the first family who saw it made an offer. That weekend, we just "happened" to find a perfect townhouse that had just gone on the market—and we bought it. Then I realized it had not been available before, so if God had helped us sell our place sooner we would not have found this wonderful home. I could have saved myself a lot of anxiety and worry if I had simply trusted God to provide exactly what we needed, when we needed it.

Anxiety and depression were undoubtedly the most common complaints among my private practice clients. I recall that those who believed in God's sovereignty and providence would often reflect on how he had never let them down in the past, as if trying to strengthen their ability to trust that he would care for them through their current circumstances. I imagine that other clinicians have noticed this pattern, since over the past decade more mental health people have begun to recognize the positive role of a strong faith in preventing and overcoming mental health challenges.

As we think about the first three beatitudes, I like John MacArthur's comparison of mourning and meekness:

> Meekness is different from being broken in spirit, though the root word is the same. In some places in the Bible these words could be used interchangeably, but I like to see a beautiful distinction. Broken in spirit focuses on my sinfulness. Meekness focuses on God's holiness. ...Broken in spirit is negative and results in mourning. Meekness is positive and results in seeking righteousness.[1]

Only when I am hungry for holiness will I allow God to mold me into the image of his Son. That is why the meek will inherit the earth, the "new earth" where "there will be no more death or mourning or crying or pain" (Revelation 21:1–4).

In the next section of this chapter we will look at our response to God's power and goodness now that we recognize the ways he has already worked in our lives.

For More Reflection

1. List some times God has intervened in your life. Thank him for taking such gentle and constant care of you.

2. Pray for the ability to see God working, or as Jesus said, to "believe the miracles" (John 10:38).

3. Think and journal about the times you faithlessly thought God did not care about your circumstances or that he was not listening to your prayers, only to later realize his solution was even better than the one you had been praying for.

4. Read the following passages to better appreciate God's unconditional love and faithfulness to his people, especially in their

times of great sinfulness: Genesis 9 (God saved Noah but he became drunk and cursed his son); Genesis 12:10–20 and Genesis 20 (God protected Abraham even when he was deceitful); Numbers 11:1–4, 16:3–41, 20:2–21:5 (God delivered Israel from Egypt but they complained and were punished, but not destroyed, again and again—he did punish various rebellious persons but never destroyed the nation); Judges 2 (God gave Israel the Promised Land, but as soon as Joshua died the Israelites took on the idolatrous practices of the Canaanites); 1 Kings 11 (Solomon had wealth, fame and wisdom, but he loved his pagan wives so much that he followed their religious practices).

Step 2: Give Up

Shadrach, Meshach and Abednego replied to the king, "O Nebuchadnezzar, we do not need to defend ourselves before you in this matter. If we are thrown into the blazing furnace, the God we serve is able to save us from it, and he will rescue us from your hand, O king. But even if he does not, we want you to know, O king, that we will not serve your gods or worship the image of gold you have set up." (Daniel 3:16–18)

It is one thing to intellectually accept that God exists, that he is the sovereign Creator, and that he hears and answers prayer, but it is quite another thing to truly rely on him throughout each day. It is the difference between saying we believe and showing our faith in action, the difference between knowing about God and knowing God.

The question is, "Who is in control?" I may say God is, but then I catch myself holding on to the reins for dear life. Personally, I have discovered that the more I try to be in control, the more God takes drastic measures to show me that I am not. In one of my favorite passages Paul learned the perils of self-reliance:

> We do not want you to be uninformed, brothers, about the hardships we suffered in the province of Asia. We were under great pressure, far beyond our ability to endure, so that we despaired even of life. Indeed, in our hearts we felt the sentence of death. But this happened that we might not rely on ourselves but on God, who raises the dead.
> (2 Corinthians 1:8–9)

Not in Control

The first step before I give up control to God, though, is to fully acknowledge that I really am not in control, and that I will never live a life of fulfillment and impact as long as I try to run the show. Unfortunately, surrender is not achieved by simply saying, "Okay, from now on I'll rely on God."

Surrender is a matter of heart as much as of behavior. I have been involved with people who had walked away from God, but later want to be restored. I recall being part of a small group working with "Barb" over a period of months. We had shown her our favorite humility scriptures, and we could see she was trying. She would say, "I really acted humble!" when describing a difficult conversation she had with her husband. The problem was that Barb's words would often belie her humility. She was quick to share her husband's faults, for example, but failed to see her own.

Fortunately, research shows that while attitude change may come before improved behavior, the reverse can also be true. This happens because when a person behaves more appropriately, they are reinforced for these positive changes (people treat them better) and then their behavior continues to change in a positive direction. So as long as Barb continues "playing the part," her heart will hopefully follow suit (especially since God will also be working to transform her from the inside out).

Often we hesitate to act until our feelings change. Consider this question: Did Shadrach, Meshach and Abednego *feel* courageous?

Scripture does not tell us, but we do know that they acted that way.

This reminds me of the angel telling Gideon he was a "mighty warrior" (Judges 6:11–40). Gideon did not feel that way about himself. Not only did he feel unprepared to lead; he was not sure God was even with his people. Gideon was a guy who would have tested my patience. First he charged that "the Lord has abandoned us," so the angel told him to "go in the strength you have."

Then Gideon argued that "my clan is the weakest in Manasseh, and I am the least in my family." Always compassionate, the Lord reassured him that "I will be with you, and you will strike down the Midianites as if they were but one man."

Of course, the story doesn't end there: Gideon was not sure God was true to his word. So he asked for a sign that it was really the Lord talking to him. He asked the Lord to wait while he went inside to prepare an offering.

When Gideon came back, the Lord caused fire to come out of a rock, consuming the meat and bread. Then Gideon realized he really was talking with God. But he still did not seem like much of a "mighty warrior." After tearing down his father's altar to Baal, which he did at night for fear of the town's men, he tested God not once but twice with the fleece. This seems to clearly disobey the command not to test God (Deuteronomy 6:16), but incredibly, God was still patient, using Gideon to powerfully defeat the Midianites.

Before we act we want God to infuse us with great faith and courage, but Jesus reminds us that "nothing will be impossible" if we simply "have faith the size of a mustard seed" (Matthew 17:20–21). Surely Gideon is a man we can imitate: we must "go in the strength we have," trusting God to do the rest.

Give Up Control

As I think about *giving up* control in order to ultimately *gain* it, I remember "Alma," a woman who came to my office complaining of multiple fears. Since venturing out on an icy day and experiencing a nasty fall, she had developed such extreme anxiety upon leaving home that it threatened her ability to go to work or even to the neighborhood market.

Like most people who are obsessed with control, much of the time Alma felt very *out* of control. Because she was compulsive about doing things perfectly, she was an excellent employee. However, at the time she first saw me she had considered a leave of absence to pursue inpatient treatment, since her fears were so intense and disabling.

Many people who come for counseling are quite lax in completing tasks suggested by the therapist, but it turned out that Alma was an excellent therapy client, compulsively performing every "homework assignment" I gave her, and in fact went beyond what I had asked.

I initially met with her twice a week. But because she gave herself completely to the therapy, within a month I was able to reduce our sessions to once a week. Within just three months after my initial meeting with Alma I had begun to see her only monthly for follow-up appointments, and she continued to progress on her own, so that in another two months she no longer needed ongoing treatment.

Alma's unusually rapid recovery was primarily due to her own willingness to trust me and surrender her own preconceived ideas and will to the therapeutic process. How much more complete is our recovery from fear when we decide to trust God and surrender our own preconceived ideas and will to the Christ-conforming process.

For More Reflection

1. Think of an experience where you really relied on God. Write about it in your journal, reflecting on how you felt before, dur-

ing and afterwards. What can you learn from this experience that will make it possible to rely on God more often?

2. On a scale of one to ten, rate how secure (safe and loved) you feel, how much you are able to endure and how deep your level of inner peace is. What can you do to close the gap between where you are and "ten" in each of these three areas?

3. In your journal, describe the circumstances where you tend to be cowardly. Now list at least three strengths you already possess that would help you overcome your fear in each of those situations. Start praying that you will remember to use these strengths the next time you are faced with one of these situations, and that God will give you the courage to act in spite of your fears.

Step 3:
Give Over

Your attitude should be the same as that of Christ Jesus:

Who, being in very nature God,
did not consider equality with God something to be grasped,
but made himself nothing,
taking the very nature of a servant,
being made in human likeness.
And being found in appearance as a man,
he humbled himself
and became obedient to death—even death on a cross!
(Philippians 2:5–8)

As Christians we are called to imitate Jesus, who chose to give over his divine rights so he could become our perfect example. But if I am really honest, the idea of becoming "less" so someone else (even Jesus) can be "greater" (John 3:30) is very challenging. My own sinful tendency is to want personal glory—not to be the suffering servant as he was. I am tempted to wonder, "Does God really expect this of me?"

Some people cop out by saying that God only wants ministers to be like Jesus. Others claim that since Jesus was God and we are just human, we could never have his motives. The question is whether truly becoming like Jesus is even a realistic goal. Obviously, God would not expect it of us if we can never achieve it, and he does expect it: "I have set you an example that you should do as I have done for you" (John 13:15).

Meekness may not be a quality people would normally strive for; nevertheless, it does bring joy: "The meek also shall increase their joy in the Lord" (Isaiah 29:19, KJV). Why is this true?

The life of Jesus is the supreme example of victory over suffering achieved by trusting God's perfect love. Jesus was perfectly secure, absolutely confident that God would never abandon him, and that God's will for him, although temporarily painful, was absolutely the best. How I long for that kind of security! John says, "There is no fear in love" (1 John 4:18). I think this means that when we are completely secure in God's love, there is nothing to fear.

Denying Ourselves

Surrender comes only when we deny or empty ourselves. Then God can fill (fulfill!) us in order to live in and through us, as we trust him to provide strength for the challenges of each day. Paul described this process in his own life:

> I have been crucified with Christ and I no longer live, but Christ lives in me. The life I live in the body, I live by faith in the Son of God, who loved me and gave himself for me. (Galatians 2:20)

This means that God is the source of anything I do that is positive or worthwhile. I cannot take credit for it, but I also no longer have to worry about being "good enough" or "measuring up."

I recently heard of a presentation given by Rick Warren, author of *The Purpose Driven Life,*[2] in which he made an interesting point about Moses. The Bible says that God tells Moses to throw down his shepherd's staff, and when he obeys, it becomes a serpent. Then, when he picks it up it becomes just an ordinary stick again.

Moses' staff can be thought of as his identity as a shepherd, his ability to influence or prod the sheep along, his profession and his livelihood. Warren talks about how God was able to do miracles with the staff only after Moses lays it down, or "surrenders" it to the Lord. But when Moses takes the staff back, it is simply a dead piece of wood.

Warren uses this illustration to encourage his audience to take whatever their "staff" is and turn it over to God for his purposes and glory. Being self-sufficient only allows us to go so far; when we surrender we will learn what God can accomplish through his power in our lives.

In his discourse about "the good shepherd," Jesus tells his disciples:

> The reason my Father loves me is that I lay down my life—only to take it up again. No one takes it from me, but I lay it down of my own accord. (John 10:17–18)

Compare this to the qualifications for being his disciple:

> If anyone would come after me, he must deny himself and take up his cross daily and follow me. For whoever wants to save his life will lose it, but whoever loses his life for me will save it. (Luke 9:23–24)

Just as Moses lays down his staff, we must surrender ourselves, laying our lives down in imitation of Jesus, if we are to experience the trust and joy in our walk with the Father that he experienced.

The acid test of a surrendered heart, though, is inner peace even in painful circumstances. This means trusting God to care for us, submitting to his will and to people—without retaliation—regardless of whether they are kind or harsh. Just as Jesus did, Peter calls us to submit:

> Slaves, submit yourselves to your masters with all respect, not only to those who are good and considerate, but also to those who are harsh. For it is commendable if a man bears up under the pain of unjust suffering because he is conscious of God. But how is it to your credit if you receive a beating for doing wrong and endure it? But if you suffer for doing good and you endure it, this is commendable before God. To this you were called, because Christ suffered for you, leaving you an example, that you should follow in his steps.
>
> "He committed no sin,
> and no deceit was found in his mouth."
>
> When they hurled their insults at him, he did not retaliate; when he suffered, he made no threats. Instead, he entrusted himself to him who judges justly. (1 Peter 2:18–23)

Victory in Self-Denial

Despite all of this, many of us are plagued by crippling fear, fear that often hinders us from living a life that can glorify God. What do we do while we are waiting for God to give us more trusting hearts? It is important to know that courage is not the absence of fear but the willingness to be empowered by entrusting ourselves to God. So, if we are eager to be used by God, he will give us the courage we need.

As always, Jesus gives us a perfect example. Matthew's account of Jesus in the Garden of Gethsemane provides a series of steps for moving forward in spite of our fear:

> Then Jesus went with his disciples to a place called Gethsemane, and he said to them, "Sit here while I go over there and pray." He took Peter and the two sons of Zebedee along with him, and he began to

> be sorrowful and troubled. Then he said to them, "My soul is overwhelmed with sorrow to the point of death. Stay here and keep watch with me."
>
> Going a little farther, he fell with his face to the ground and prayed, "My Father, if it is possible, may this cup be taken from me. Yet not as I will, but as you will."
>
> Then he returned to his disciples and found them sleeping. "Could you men not keep watch with me for one hour?" he asked Peter. "Watch and pray so that you will not fall into temptation. The spirit is willing but the body is weak."
>
> He went away a second time and prayed, "My Father, if it is not possible for this cup to be taken away unless I drink it, may your will be done."
>
> When he came back, he again found them sleeping, because their eyes were heavy. So he left them and went away once more and prayed the third time, saying the same thing.
>
> Then he returned to the disciples and said to them, "Are you still sleeping and resting? Look, the hour is near, and the Son of Man is betrayed into the hands of sinners. Rise, let us go! Here comes my betrayer!" (Matthew 26:36–46)

I love Jesus' humanity here: even he was gripped by terror—a fear so intense that his sweat fell like drops of blood (Luke 22:44). We find it hard to die to ourselves even though we are not facing the torture of a physical cross and separation from God! Fortunately, Jesus does not give in to panic or paralysis. Instead, he

- Seeks out the support of his closest friends
- Gets open, sharing his struggle
- Begs God for strength
- Keeps praying again and again (three times!)—until his inner peace and resolve are restored
- Is compassionate (rather than bitter) when his friends let him down (by sleeping at his most challenging time)

- Continues to provide spiritual guidance despite his own struggles
- Takes decisive action after receiving strength from God

Jesus is the supreme example of submission to God and, in doing so, entrusting himself to God's will. We are told that for "the joy set before him, he endured the cross" and ultimately "sat down at the right hand of the throne of God" (Hebrews 12:2). Trust and surrender bring joy and fulfillment." I think trust always precedes surrender so I put it first.

For More Reflection

1. Close your eyes and imagine acting courageously in a situation where you are often immobilized by fear. Then journal about how it usually feels to be faced with this situation and how it felt to be courageous.

2. Reflect on Hebrews 12:2–4. Write your reactions in your journal, thinking about specific ways to follow Jesus' example in growing more courageous.

3. Write about how the action you typically take when you are fearful is like, or not like, each of the ways Jesus reacted in the Garden of Gethsemane. Make a plan for developing stronger spiritual relationships: although Jesus' friends let him down in the Garden, God wants us to strengthen each other in challenging times (for example, see Romans 1:12, Romans 15:14, 2 Corinthians 1:3–7, and Colossians 3:16).

❄

As our reward for meekness, we will "inherit the earth." What does this mean? First, those who are truly meek and gentle will enjoy the best life this world brings. The more I trust God and surrender to his will, the more secure I can be with *whatever* happens, confident that he is there to help and care for me. My relationships are better too: I am not in control of other people, but I can relax because God *is*. In other words, when I imitate the meekness of Jesus, I am content and at rest (Matthew 11:29).

This promise may also refer to "the new earth" described in Revelation 21. Jesus says that, in the new Jerusalem

> "...the dwelling of God is with men, and he will live with them. They will be his people, and God himself will be with them and be their God. He will wipe every tear from their eyes. There will be no more death or mourning or crying or pain, for the old order of things has passed away." (vv3–4)

If I am meek and surrendered, I will be there! This sounds so incredible that I want it *now*, and that hunger is exactly what we need to feel as we move to the next chapter.

5

Hunger

Commit to Spiritual Growth

"Blessed are those who hunger and thirst for righteousness,
for they will be filled."

Matthew 5:6

Righteousness. The word evokes a saintliness, an image of someone in a flowing white robe who is above the normal challenges of life, who "walks on water" while the rest of us scurry around like little mice looking for a tidbit of food. It is interesting that Jesus did not say, "Blessed are the righteous"; he said "blessed are those who hunger and thirst for righteousness." Righteousness is holiness, goodness, virtue or integrity. Some people say it means "being right with God," but this definition does not indicate an ongoing spiritual growth. While following the biblical plan of salvation makes us right with God, if we become more and more like Jesus, we will gradually be "sanctified"—our righteousness will continue to grow for the rest of our lives.

There is a big difference, though, between those who are aware of how far they need to go in their personal righteousness, and those who think they have already arrived. I recall a coworker telling me, "Her problem is that she's so righteous!" when referring to someone we knew who thought she was righteous. "Self-righteous" is the term some use for this kind of person. Although my coworker misused the word "righteous," the Bible has a lot to say about being truly righteous, and about being self-deceived. Jesus rebuked the Pharisees for their pride—for thinking they were righteous:

> Woe to you, teachers of the law and Pharisees, you hypocrites! You are like whitewashed tombs, which look beautiful on the outside but on the inside are full of dead men's bones and everything unclean. In the same way, on the outside you appear to people as righteous but on the inside you are full of hypocrisy and wickedness. (Matthew 23:27–28)

What about the real thing—being truly righteous? First, the rewards of righteousness far outweigh the sacrifices it may cost:

> The LORD rewards every man for his righteousness and faithfulness. (1 Samuel 26:23)

> The fruit of righteousness will be peace;
> the effect of righteousness will be quietness and confidence forever.
> (Isaiah 32:17)

Next, we need not wonder what God wants us to do, since he provides us with direction:

> He guides me in paths of righteousness for his name's sake. (Psalm 23:3)

> If you need wisdom—if you want to know what God wants you to do—ask him, and he will gladly tell you. He will not resent your asking. (James 1:5, NLT)

Finally, it is God who will give you the passion and ability to grow in righteousness. We will always fall short, but through the intervention of God's Spirit we can overcome much of the sin that prevents us from living a life that pleases and glorifies God:

> Sow for yourselves righteousness,
> reap the fruit of unfailing love,
> and break up your unplowed ground;
> for it is time to seek the LORD,
> until he comes
> and showers righteousness on you. (Hosea 10:12)

This passage makes it clear that true righteousness comes from God, but what can we do to prepare ourselves by "sowing righteousness"?

- Experience Emptiness: Fully acknowledge that life is meaningless without God
- Experience Earnestness: Immerse ourselves in the Bible, since it is there that we find all the answers and inspiration we need
- Experience Emancipation: Continue putting God's word into practice, celebrating the freedom that comes from building our lives on the rock (Matthew 7:24).

To claim Jesus' promise that those who hunger and thirst for righteousness will be filled, we must…

Commit to Spiritual Growth

Step 1: Experience Emptiness

Jesus continued: "There was a man who had two sons. The younger one said to his father, 'Father, give me my share of the estate.' So he divided his property between them.

"Not long after that, the younger son got together all he had, set off for a distant country and there squandered his wealth in wild living. After he had spent everything, there was a severe famine in that whole country, and he began to be in need. So he went and hired himself out to a citizen of that country, who sent him to his fields to feed pigs. He longed to fill his stomach with the pods that the pigs were eating, but no one gave him anything.

"When he came to his senses, he said, 'How many of my father's hired men have food to spare, and here I am starving to death! I will set out and go back to my father and say to him: Father, I have sinned against heaven and against you. I am no longer worthy to be called

> your son; make me like one of your hired men.' So he got up and went to his father.
>
> "But while he was still a long way off, his father saw him and was filled with compassion for him; he ran to his son, threw his arms around him and kissed him.
>
> "The son said to him, 'Father, I have sinned against heaven and against you. I am no longer worthy to be called your son.'
>
> "But the father said to his servants, 'Quick! Bring the best robe and put it on him. Put a ring on his finger and sandals on his feet. Bring the fattened calf and kill it. Let's have a feast and celebrate. For this son of mine was dead and is alive again; he was lost and is found.' So they began to celebrate." (Luke 15:11–24)

The rebellious young man in this story did not appreciate the life he had at home. He thought he could find a better life out on his own, away from the influence and control of his father. In the same way, it is easy for us to be lured by the glamour and apparent freedom of the world around us. We may be tempted to escape from the restrictions imposed by our Heavenly Father, the "thou shalt nots" of the Christian faith. Only when we have experienced the emptiness of living without God can we begin to appreciate the true freedom that Jesus offers.

There is a similar parallel in the counseling world. Therapists recognize that whether or not a new client will benefit from counseling is directly related to the degree of emotional pain they are experiencing. While a new therapist in private practice, I saw "Frances" as one of my first clients. In our first session she reported having been unhappy in her marriage for at least ten years. She had also been involved in a clandestine extramarital affair during that time. This should have been my first clue: if she had tolerated her unhappiness and waited that long to seek help, it was unlikely that she would now make the necessary sacrifices required to truly change.

As it turned out, despite seeing her individually and with her husband weekly for almost a year, Frances' discomfort was simply not severe enough to provide the needed motivation and willingness to risk telling her husband the truth. Although Frances was definitely not "happy," despite my trying to convince her that her life could be so much more, her existence was familiar and she preferred to keep it that way rather than risk losing the security of home and marriage.

The Empty Life

The rebellious young man had definitely come to the point of seeing how empty his life was as he sought to live it according to his own desires.

Solomon conducted an experiment to find out what really brings happiness. In the second chapter of Ecclesiastes, he records his results: having fun, working hard and seeking wisdom are all meaningless without God.

> The best that people can do is eat, drink, and enjoy their work. I saw that even this comes from God, because no one can eat or enjoy life without him. If people please God, God will give them wisdom, knowledge, and joy. But sinners will get only the work of gathering and storing wealth that they will have to give to the ones who please God. So all their work is useless, like chasing the wind. (Ecclesiastes 2:24–26, NCV)

At times I wonder why so many of us refuse to live God's way; after all, what do we have to lose? One answer is that we are enticed by the things the world offers. Satan's ploy is to make us think life would be better or more fun if we denied—or ignored—God. Ask yourself: do you secretly envy those who are "rich and famous," who live their lives as if they don't care what anyone (including God) thinks? Have there been times you have wandered—or run—away from God because his way was too hard or you were impatient for his help? No matter how faithful we are, if we are honest with ourselves, most of us will admit we have at least considered this. Asaph, a prophet who served under King David, records his struggle in Psalm 73:

> But as for me, my feet had almost slipped;
> I had nearly lost my foothold.
> For I envied the arrogant
> when I saw the prosperity of the wicked.
> They have no struggles;
> their bodies are healthy and strong. (Psalm 73:2–4)

He goes on to lament the blessings enjoyed by the wicked, but eventually comes to his senses:

> Surely you place them on slippery ground;
> you cast them down to ruin.
> How suddenly are they destroyed,
> completely swept away by terrors!
> As a dream when one awakes,
> so when you arise, O LORD,
> you will despise them as fantasies.
>
> When my heart was grieved
> and my spirit embittered,
> I was senseless and ignorant;
> I was a brute beast before you.
>
> Yet I am always with you;
> you hold me by my right hand.
> You guide me with your counsel,
> and afterward you will take me into glory.
> Whom have I in heaven but you?
> And earth has nothing I desire besides you.
> My flesh and my heart may fail,
> but God is the strength of my heart
> and my portion forever. (Psalm 73:18–26)

The last few verses of this passage inspire us because they express the kind of devotion we long for, and also because they are written by a man we can relate to, who had his spiritual lows as well as his mountain-top highs.

Filling the Emptiness

God has created in every person a hunger to know him, although we may allow worldliness or a false sense of security to numb us from the emptiness of our lives. Well-meaning counselors attempt to "treat" that emptiness with a variety of therapies.

I hate to admit that I was once one of those counselors! I remember clients who were clearly in this kind of spiritual crisis, but since I was unprepared to provide biblical guidance, I used the tools I had in my "psychological toolbox." Occasionally, my listening helped them recognize the true source of their emptiness. At that point, though, I was unable to guide them further other than to suggest they speak with a pastor.

Our loving Father has designed this hunger of the soul to drive the non-Christian to seek to know him. Later, after conversion, the awareness that we are not meeting God's standard creates an emptiness that we fill by becoming more like Jesus. Peter says that because we have been given his "great and precious promises" and have been allowed to "participate in the divine nature," we should

> Make every effort to add to [our] faith goodness; and to goodness, knowledge; and to knowledge, self-control; and to self-control, perseverance; and to perseverance, godliness; and to godliness, brotherly kindness; and to brotherly kindness, love. For if [we] possess these qualities in increasing measure, they will keep [us] from being ineffective and unproductive in [our] knowledge of our Lord Jesus Christ. (2 Peter 1:5–8)

For More Reflection

1. What are the things you use to "numb out"? Answer this question in your journal: What keeps me from facing my own emptiness and need for God?

2. Reflect on the following quote from Martin Seligman's book *Authentic Happiness*: "Positive emotion alienated from the exercise of character leads to emptiness, to inauthenticity, to depression, and, as we age, to the gnawing realization that we are fidgeting until we die."[1] Do you agree or disagree with this quote—in your own life, the lives of people you know, and those of the "rich and famous"?

3. Write the answer to this question: What can keep me from really going after my relationship with God—from making it my first priority?

Step 2: Experience Earnestness

O God, you are my God,
earnestly I seek you;
my soul thirsts for you,
my body longs for you,
in a dry and weary land
where there is no water. (Psalm 63:1)

When David wrote this psalm, he was living the life of an outlaw in the desert, being pursued by King Saul who was trying to kill him. Although the Bible does not provide much detail about how David and his men coped with desert life, the verse refers to "a dry and weary land where there is no water." David undoubtedly knew physical thirst, but more importantly, he experienced spiritual thirst: "my soul thirsts for you, my body longs for you."

Most of us cannot imagine the physical pain and desperation

that result from being deprived of water for an extended period. In the Western world, we enjoy refrigerators that dispense ice and water (purified!) at the touch of a button, bottled water and even little packets of flavoring to make our water tastier. But the downside of these conveniences is that we may fail to appreciate what God is really communicating about the driving power of thirst.

As I studied "thirst" in preparation for writing this chapter, I was astounded by the number of passages that refer to water. The Bible portrays God as a fountain of life from whom flows an inexhaustible supply of living water. This living water cleanses us from sin (Zechariah 13:1, 1 Peter 3:21), enables us to bear fruit (Ezekiel 47:12), brings continual blessing (Psalm 36:8), leads to peace and righteousness (Isaiah 48:18) and results in eternal life (John 4:14). God warns us not to abandon him and instead dig our own "broken cisterns that cannot hold water" (Jeremiah 2:13). In Revelation 21:6, Jesus says:

> It is done. I am the Alpha and the Omega, the Beginning and the End. To him who is thirsty I will give to drink without cost from the spring of the water of life.

And in Revelation 22:17:

> The Spirit and the bride say, "Come!" And let him who hears say, "Come!" Whoever is thirsty, let him come; and whoever wishes, let him take the free gift of the water of life.

God longs to shower us with blessing, but we must first love, trust and obey him. David feared for his very life, but his reliance on God sustained him. During the dark period when he was running from Saul, he wrote

> Because your love is better than life,
>   my lips will glorify you...
> My soul will be satisfied as with the richest of foods;
>   with singing lips my mouth will praise you. (Psalm 63:3, 5)

David's relationship with God was not "optional"—it was more than precious, his very source of survival.

The Importance of Being Earnest

Exactly how does God want us to be earnest? Throughout the Bible, he commands us to be wholehearted, zealous, sincere, devoted, impassioned and urgent, while he warns against apathy, nonchalance, being unenthusiastic, halfhearted or lukewarm. Jesus sums it up in the following words:

> "'Hear, O Israel, the Lord our God, the Lord is one. Love the Lord your God with all your heart and with all your soul and with all your mind and with all your strength.' The second is this: 'Love your neighbor as yourself.' There is no commandment greater than these." (Mark 12:29–31)

We might think of the book of Deuteronomy as the "wholehearted book." In it, Moses writes that we are to apply our "whole hearts" to the following aspects of our relationship with God:

- Seeking him (4:29)
- Loving him (6:5)
- Serving him (10:12)
- Observing his commands (26:16)
- Obeying him (30:2)
- Turning to him (30:10)

Many people respond to their hunger for God by becoming "religious," never learning that the answers for victorious living can only come from his word. These folks will quickly tell you that the Bible is the inspired word of God, but the truth is that they rarely read it. Sure, they go to church each Sunday, expecting the pastor to impart some wisdom from the Scriptures to get them through the week. How much better would their lives work, and how much more would they be blessed, if they invested half the time feasting on God's word that they typically spend—or waste—watching TV. (Realize that reading the Bible is an investment in yourself, your family and your future.)

Studying the Scriptures is a practical way to demonstrate our commitment to living God's way. We may pray, but if we want to have a two-way conversation with God, we must read his word, since this is one of the major ways he gives us the answers we are seeking. In my times with God, I usually pray first. At the end of my prayer, I ask God for answers to my questions about current challenges in my life. I am always amazed at how often I "just happen to" find answers that day in the Bible passage I am reading.

If I am struggling with a particular sin or life challenge, I find it helpful to see what the Bible says about that. Many great study Bibles are available, but I especially love my *Thompson Chain Reference Bible.* I begin by looking in the concordance for a particular word. Next, I go to a scripture listed in the concordance. Then I look in the margin next to the scripture for the number referring to the location for that topic in the chain index and—voila!—I often find an entire study on that particular topic. Finally, there are free computer sites for Bible study, such as BibleGateway.com or Crosswalk.com.

Sometimes people ask if it matters what version of the Bible they read. Some translations may in fact be more accurate, word-for-word reflections of the original Hebrew and Greek manuscripts. Others believe a certain translation (such as the King James) is the only "true" Bible. I believe that whichever translation increases our ability to understand the Scriptures and then put them into practice will be the best version for us. Also, Web sites such as BibleGateway.com make it possible to compare multiple translations of the same passage, and also to search various commentaries for more explanation or scholarly reviews.

One question remains before we move on: Why is reading the

Bible so essential? Let's turn to the Scriptures themselves for the answer. Following are my favorite "Top Ten" reasons for regular Bible study:

- Scripture is the perfect foundation for our lives:

> "Therefore everyone who hears these words of mine and puts them into practice is like a wise man who built his house on the rock." (Matthew 7:24)

- Scripture fully equips us for living:

> All Scripture is God-breathed and is useful for teaching, rebuking, correcting and training in righteousness, so that the man of God may be thoroughly equipped for every good work. (2 Timothy 3:16–17)

- The Word is our "sword" for fighting off Satan's attacks:

> Take the helmet of salvation and the sword of the Spirit, which is the word of God. (Ephesians 6:17)

- We need the Scriptures for spiritual survival:

> He humbled you, causing you to hunger and then feeding you with manna, which neither you nor your fathers had known, to teach you that man does not live on bread alone but on every word that comes from the mouth of the LORD. (Deuteronomy 8:3)

- Reading the Bible increases our faith:

> Consequently, faith comes from hearing the message, and the message is heard through the word of Christ. (Romans 10:17)

- The Scriptures are a guide, lighting our way in a dark world:

> Your word is a lamp to my feet
>   and a light for my path. (Psalm 119:105)

- Our thinking will be faulty without the truth of God's word:

Jesus replied, "You are in error because you do not know the Scriptures or the power of God." (Matthew 22:29)

- The Scriptures are necessary for spiritual growth:

Like newborn babies, crave pure spiritual milk, so that by it you may grow up in your salvation. (1 Peter 2:2)

- Over time, we are purified (made holy) by reading and following the word:

"Sanctify them by the truth; your word is truth." (John 17:17)

- God will judge us by the standards set forth in his word:

"There is a judge for the one who rejects me and does not accept my words; that very word which I spoke will condemn him at the last day." (John 12:48)

For More Reflection

1. Read Psalm 42:1–2. In your journal, reflect on what it would take to develop this kind of thirst for intimacy with God.

2. Make a list of all the benefits of God's word mentioned by the writer of Psalm 119.

3. Does your level of "craving" for God motivate you to nibble, to take a bite from, or to feast on his word? Discuss with a spiritual friend: Which sins might be revealed by a lack of earnestness (unbelief, idolatry, pride, laziness, worldliness, etc.)? What can you do to repent of the sins that keep you from going deeper in your relationship with God?

Step 3: Experience Emancipation

To the Jews who had believed him, Jesus said, "If you hold to my

> teaching, you are really my disciples. Then you will know the truth, and the truth will set you free." (John 8:31–32)

Philosophers throughout the ages have searched for truth. But Jesus makes an incredible promise to his followers: continuing to follow his teachings will result not only in knowledge of the truth, but also in the freedom that comes from that truth. Do we really appreciate the value of this promise? Do we realize we need to be set free? Without even realizing it, you may be enslaved, in bondage. So the question becomes, "From what can Jesus set us free?"

- Fear and insecurity:

> Be content with what you have, because God has said,
>
> "Never will I leave you;
> never will I forsake you."
>
> So we say with confidence,
>
> "The Lord is my helper; I will not be afraid.
> What can man do to me?" (Hebrews 13:5b–6)

- Anxiety:

> Cast all your anxiety on him because he cares for you. (1 Peter 5:7)

- Worry:

> "Therefore I tell you, do not worry about your life, what you will eat or drink; or about your body, what you will wear. Is not life more important than food, and the body more important than clothes? Look at the birds of the air; they do not sow or reap or store away in barns, and yet your heavenly Father feeds them. Are you not much more valuable than they? Who of you by worrying can add a single hour to his life?" (Matthew 6:25–27)

- Guilt:

> Let us draw near to God with a sincere heart in full assurance of faith, having our hearts sprinkled to cleanse us from a guilty conscience and having our bodies washed with pure water. (Hebrews 10:22)

- Discouragement and depression:

> The LORD is close to the brokenhearted
> and saves those who are crushed in spirit. (Psalm 34:18)

- Sin:

> Therefore, there is now no condemnation for those who are in Christ Jesus, because through Christ Jesus the law of the Spirit of life set me free from the law of sin and death. (Romans 8:1–2)

Despite the encouragement found in the above passages, though, someone caught in the grip of anxiety or depression is not usually miraculously "cured" by simply reading that God loves him and will never leave him. So a better question is: How can we claim the promise Jesus makes in John 8:31?

Consider the audience to whom Jesus addressed this amazing claim: the Jews who had believed him. Obviously, many of the Jews had not believed Jesus, seeing him as just another charlatan claiming to be divine. But the people who listened to Jesus this day were believers, probably hanging on Jesus' every word—looking for answers and for validation that they, of all Jews, had found the Messiah.

Rather than praising them for their faith, in essence Jesus says, "It's not enough to just believe—you have to keep on believing and practicing my teachings." Some translations insert the word "obey" in this passage. For example, the *New Living Translation* reads: "if you keep obeying my teachings." The *Amplified Bible* translates this passage:

> "If you abide in My word [hold fast to My teachings and live in accordance with them], you are truly My disciples." (John 8:31)

I know from personal experience the freedom that results from walking with Jesus. As a younger woman I was full of insecurities. I was easily intimidated. Whenever I felt "exposed" when speaking in public or meeting someone I considered a superior, my anxiety was so intense that I would stutter or lose my ability to think clearly. I would imagine people were talking about me behind my back, and I envied anyone who appeared confident. I believed in Jesus, went to church, and read the Bible, but obedience was a problem: like many insecure people I avoided scriptures that I thought would only increase my guilt and decrease my self-esteem.

It was not until I willingly surrendered to the influence of loving Christian women who taught me how to live the Bible each day that I began, over time, to be freed from my fears, insecurity and anxiety. No longer enslaved by them, I began to see my insecurities as evidence of unbelief, self-reliance and even idolatry (looking to people for approval rather than living to please God).

I began to take practical steps: studying scriptures specifically related to my struggle, begging God for strength and guidance, asking others to pray for me and exercising the faith I did have to take small risks in order to develop my "spiritual muscles."

I cannot say that I never feel insecure nowadays, but these feelings definitely come less often. Most important, when they do come, I am still able to function and recognize them for what they are: Satan's attempt to prevent me from doing the things God wants me to do. As long as I respond in a spiritual way—by praying and getting help—these times can be an opportunity for growth, and I am able to experience the emancipation that Jesus offers.

Freedom is actually what people seek from professional counseling, and modern therapeutic approaches are intended to provide that freedom. Cognitive-behavioral approaches may free a client from the tyranny of his irrational beliefs and behaviors. Drug treatments, including *anti*depressant, *anti*anxiety and *anti*psychotic medications, are formulated to free the sufferer from the symptoms of depression, anxiety or psychosis. Psychodynamic therapy is used to free people from their unconscious conflicts; family systems therapies free them from dysfunctional family relationships; and humanistic therapy is supposed to free people from self-limiting patterns.

What about these therapies? As a psychologist, I can honestly say that, while these therapies may have some value, I believe that only God can offer *true freedom*—the kind of freedom that results in a life of contentment, inner peace and joy.

For More Reflection

1. In John 10:10, Jesus says he came to give us "life to the full." What would this life be like? In your journal, describe this full life as you imagine it. Really let your imagination go. Begin with the phrase, "I'm sitting in my _______ and I'm thinking..."
2. On a scale of one to ten, rate your "earnestness"—how wholehearted you are in your commitment to spiritual growth. Consider how often you pray and study your Bible, how willing you are to ask spiritual friends for input and help, and how much you are willing to take risks to share your faith with others.
3. If you are not experiencing the freedom that Jesus offers, what is standing in your way? Make a plan to study what the Bible says about the sins or obstacles in your life that prevent you from claiming Jesus' promise.

❄

God will not disappoint us if, in our heart of hearts, we long to be righteous. Jesus says we will be filled if we hunger *and* thirst—so clearly our discontent can only be satisfied by a growing intimacy with the living God. In fact, this continuous communion with God will be needed to adopt his heart of compassion—which brings us to the next chapter.

6

Mercy

Overflow with Compassion

"Blessed are the merciful,
for they will be shown mercy."
Matthew 5:7

Humility, brokenness, surrender, a passion for God. These are inward traits producing a special kind of outward response toward other people. God never intended for us to be hermits, to live our lives separated from others. Instead, he commands that we love our neighbors as we do ourselves, and this next attribute—mercy—is the expression of that love. If there is one thing that defined Christ, it was his compassionate love. His love is what set him apart from the religious people of his day.

Jesus expressed his love in words: "As the Father has loved me, so I have loved you. Now remain in my love" (John 15:9). He expressed it in action: "Having loved his own who were in the world, he now showed them the full extent of his love" (John 13:1b).

While Jesus loved his disciples, he also showed great compassion for those who might never follow his way:

> When he saw the crowds, he had compassion on them, because they were harassed and helpless, like sheep without a shepherd. (Matthew 9:36)

> "O Jerusalem, Jerusalem, you who kill the prophets and stone those sent to you, how often I have longed to gather your children together, as a hen gathers her chicks under her wings, but you were not willing." (Matthew 23:37)

> Jesus looked at him and loved him. "One thing you lack," he said. "Go, sell everything you have and give to the poor, and you will have treasure in heaven. Then come, follow me."
>
> At this the man's face fell. He went away sad, because he had great wealth. (Mark 10:21–22)

Jesus even loved those who would ultimately torture and kill him:

> But God demonstrates his own love for us in this: While we were still sinners, Christ died for us. (Romans 5:8)

To be merciful is to be kind. Other synonyms include gentleness, graciousness, forgiveness, generosity and softheartedness. I am meant to soothe, to heal with my words, my touch, my attention and even my facial expression—whether or not the person who is hurting is my friend.

More than twenty years ago, while a staff psychologist at a hospital for children with special needs, I had the great pleasure of working with "Tammy," a thirteen-year-old girl with multiple disabilities including cerebral palsy and a life-threatening heart-lung defect. Because of her weak heart, she was unable to participate even in slightly strenuous activities. I recall playing air hockey with her one day in the hospital recreation room, and despite loving the game, after five minutes she became so winded that she had to rest.

Tammy needed surgery to repair her heart, a procedure with only a fifty-percent survival rate. Since her struggles had made her mature beyond her years, her parents believed that whether to have the surgery should be her decision. My role was to help her think through the pros and cons.

One day while we were involved in an especially "heavy" conversation, my son, Greg, called in tears because he "just knew" he'd failed the test he'd taken that day in his tenth-grade math class. The secretary wouldn't disturb us except in an emergency, but Greg was in such a state that she put him through.

I interrupted my session with Tammy, and as I began to reassure him, Tammy said, "Let me speak to him!" She had never met or talked with Greg, but she knew I had a son in high school. Not knowing what to expect but not wanting to refuse her, I handed her the phone.

She introduced herself, and in her best "therapeutic voice" (imitating me, I suppose), she told Greg to take a deep breath and began to teach him the relaxation technique I'd taught her for handling her anxiety. Here was a girl in the throes of a life-and-death decision who put her own concerns aside to help a total stranger.

Tammy decided to have the surgery, and when I visited her in the ICU, she was still consoling the people around her. Although she passed away a few days later, her healing influence was still very much alive: at her funeral, everyone agreed that she'd been a very special girl whose life had made a healing impact.

In Jeremiah 8:22 God is referred to as a "balm," a healing salve or ointment applied to a wound. In the same way, Christ healed our wounds (see Isaiah 53:5), and we are to heal the wounds of others (1 John 3:16). To have a healing influence, we must first...

Overflow with Compassion

Although I long to be more like Jesus, I always seem to fall short in this area. It is so much easier for me to be insensitive, selfish, hard-hearted, abrasive or irritable, especially with those who dislike or disagree with me. Fortunately, God's word provides specific steps for us to follow in order to grow in our compassion:

- Allow Him to Connect with You: Acknowledging our insufficiency, we must continue to reach out for his mercy and help.
- Allow Him to Empower You: Jesus enables us to love, giving us a heart of mercy and forgiveness even when this may seem

unreasonable to the outside world.

- Allow Him to Move You: God's Spirit propels us into acts of compassion even when that is not our "nature."

We need to maintain our connection to Jesus. We must remember that we continually need his mercy in our own lives.

Step 1: Allow Him to Connect with You

"I am the vine; you are the branches. If a man remains in me and I in him, he will bear much fruit; apart from me you can do nothing." (John 15:5)

Jesus wants to connect with us, taking the initiative by calling us into fellowship with him. And, as he often did, he added an incentive: remaining in him would result in much fruit—the fruit of his Spirit (see Galatians 5:22–23) as well as a harvest of souls. If we want God to bless us with this kind of fruit, it is essential to know what "remaining" in him really means.

We start out being "in Christ" at the time of our conversion:

If anyone is in Christ, he is a new creation; the old has gone, the new has come! (2 Corinthians 5:17)

Over time, we grow to know him better:

And we pray this in order that you may live a life worthy of the Lord and may please him in every way: bearing fruit in every good work, growing in the knowledge of God, being strengthened with all power according to his glorious might. (Colossians 1:10–11)

I keep asking that the God of our Lord Jesus Christ, the glorious Father, may give you the Spirit of wisdom and revelation, so that you may know him better. (Ephesians 1:17)

Remaining in him also entails ongoing confession of sin and

repentance, to God in the privacy of our prayer times, and to spiritual friends who can advise and pray for us (see James 5:16). This is not something that is "done with" at the time of our baptism, but part of a lifelong commitment to Christian growth:

> If we claim to have fellowship with him yet walk in the darkness, we lie and do not live by the truth. But if we walk in the light, as he is in the light, we have fellowship with one another, and the blood of Jesus, his Son, purifies us from all sin.
>
> If we claim to be without sin, we deceive ourselves and the truth is not in us. If we confess our sins, he is faithful and just and will forgive us our sins and purify us from all unrighteousness. If we claim we have not sinned, we make him out to be a liar and his word has no place in our lives. (1 John 1:6–10)

Although confession of sin can be embarrassing, especially for an older Christian who "should know better," it reminds us that we can never look down on anyone since, after all, we would all be lost without God's grace.

Growing in our fellowship with Jesus through confession is the primary way to overflow with compassion and mercy: in our natural, sinful state, we are tempted to be critical and judgmental, especially after we have come to know Christ. It is easy to think that we have all the answers, and that if others would listen to us or do things our way, they would be better off. But when we acknowledge, on an ongoing basis, how far we are from God's perfect standard, we see the truth of Jesus' claim that "apart from me you can do nothing," and we are more patient and forgiving with the imperfections of others.

Love Your Enemies

Being compassionate toward people who are hurting may be easy, but our compassion is really tested when someone hurts us, especially when that injury was intentional. We may know we should "love our enemies and pray for those who persecute us"

(Matthew 5:44), but this characteristic of Jesus can be one of the most difficult to imitate.

I have recently had an opportunity to learn this firsthand. After leaving a management position where my supervisor's demands had become intolerable, I filed for unemployment benefits while searching for a new job. My former employer claimed I did not deserve these benefits, and despite my having gone "beyond the call of duty" in the three years I worked there and having represented my case truthfully, the company continued to claim I resigned without good cause.

Eventually, the case was resolved in their favor, so I had to repay three months worth of benefits. To put it mildly, this seemed unjust to me. I struggled not to sin by being angry and bitter, and for a time found it very difficult to be compassionate toward these people who were trying to prevent me from collecting what I felt was lawfully mine.

I finally realized, though, that God had given me a perfect opportunity to practice what I preach! I asked myself, "What would I say to someone else in this situation?" The answer was clear: relent, forgive and guard against holding a grudge (Matthew 5:40, Matthew 18:21–22, 1 Corinthians 13:5). Although these are hard lessons to learn, I am grateful that God uses even these painful experiences for good.

Victims of childhood abuse may find it especially difficult to forgive. Sometimes there is a desire to forgive the abuser, but the act of forgiving and letting go is complicated by the victim's own underlying feeling of guilt—that somehow she must have caused the abuse or should have been able to stop it.

To the victim, forgiveness feels as if she is saying, "It's okay that the abuse happened," when in fact it can never be okay. The victim also irrationally believes that holding on to her anger or hatred constitutes punishment that the abuser deserves, so letting go of that anger would be unjust.

Growing up, "Pamela" was molested by her stepdad and uncle for fourteen years. Never able to confide in her mother, she carried this "dirty secret" throughout her teen years. As an adult, she still struggles with the unfairness of having been robbed of a normal childhood, and at times finds it difficult to believe that God could possibly love her.

She resists any suggestion that she needs to take some responsibility for her own recovery because she equates this with the thought that she was responsible for the abuse itself. This is all the more complicated because the relationship with her stepfather was both negative *and* positive, especially since it's easier to view the world in black or white terms. Until Pamela is able to complete the past, experiencing gratitude for the ways her stepfather was *there* for her, along with forgiveness for the ways he hurt her, she will find it difficult to move forward to pursue a mature marriage relationship.

Jesus made it very clear that we will be forgiven only to the extent that we are willing to forgive others:

> "For if you forgive men when they sin against you, your heavenly Father will also forgive you. But if you do not forgive men their sins, your Father will not forgive your sins." (Matthew 6:14–15)

Does this mean he does not understand or is insensitive to the pain of abuse?

Jesus may not have experienced the type of abuse that we have, but he definitely knows what it is to be abused—both mentally and physically. The soldiers beat him until his skin was lacerated. They hit him on the head, causing the crown of thorns to puncture his skin again and again. They forced him to carry his cross on shoulders that were already raw and bloody. They hammered nails through his wrists and feet, and then they elevated the cross, causing him unimaginable torture as he was forced to push up on the nails in his feet with every breath. He was spit on, laughed at and humiliated. But Jesus never responded with hatred or retaliation, but instead cried out, "Father, forgive them, for they do not know what they are doing" (Luke 23:34).

Although most of us will never experience anything like Jesus did, this is not to minimize the trauma suffered by modern victims, particularly those who were sexually abused as children. In a sense, sexual abuse is "abuse times three"—mental, physical *and* sexual—so it is that much more horrific. Does God really understand and if so, why would he allow someone he loves to experience such agony?

When David's son Amnon raped his sister Tamar, the Bible records that she responded as follows:

> Tamar put ashes on her head and tore the ornamented robe she was wearing. She put her hand on her head and went away, weeping aloud as she went.
>
> Her brother Absalom said to her, "Has that Amnon, your brother, been with you? Be quiet now, my sister; he is your brother. Don't take this thing to heart." And Tamar lived in her brother Absalom's house, a desolate woman. (2 Samuel 13:19–20)

What does it mean to be "desolate"? *Roget's New Millennium Thesaurus* contains the following note:

> "Lonely" adds to "solitary" a suggestion of longing for companionship, while "lonesome" heightens the suggestion of sadness; "forlorn" and "desolate" are even more isolated and sad.

We do not know what became of Tamar, but it is unlikely that she ever married since in Old Testament culture a woman who was raped was considered forever disgraced and defiled. If we have been abused, we have the choice of either forgiving the abuser or of being "a desolate woman" who is held captive by her own lack of forgiveness.

God understands and mourns the pain of abuse. At the same time, he can be glorified when we overcome (that is, overpower) the abuse by forgiving and letting go, since refusing to forgive our abusers only gives abusive acts a continuing hold on us.

Joseph was betrayed by his brothers, stripped and thrown into an empty cistern, and sold to the Ishmaelites for twenty shekels of silver. Later, he was falsely accused of attempted rape by Potiphar's wife and imprisoned for more than two years.

After all he went through, Joseph had every reason to be bitter, but the Bible records the following interaction when he was finally reunited with his brothers after many years:

> Joseph said to his brothers, "I am Joseph! Is my father still living?" But his brothers were not able to answer him, because they were terrified at his presence.
>
> Then Joseph said to his brothers, "Come close to me." When they had done so, he said, "I am your brother Joseph, the one you sold into Egypt! And now, do not be distressed and do not be angry with yourselves for selling me here, because it was to save lives that God sent me ahead of you. For two years now there has been famine in the land, and for the next five years there will not be plowing and reaping. But God sent me ahead of you to preserve for you a remnant on earth and to save your lives by a great deliverance.
>
> "So then, it was not you who sent me here, but God. He made me father to Pharaoh, lord of his entire household and ruler of all Egypt." (Genesis 45:3–8)

Joseph did not allow his brothers' actions to drag him into the sin of hatred. This is a huge temptation whenever we are mistreated. Although the responsibility for the abuse belongs completely to the abuser, if we respond with anger, hatred, or bitterness—toward the abuser or toward God—we must take responsibility for that sin. It is comforting to know that Jesus understands from personal experience our temptation:

> For we do not have a high priest who is unable to sympathize with our

weaknesses, but we have one who has been tempted in every way, just as we are—yet was without sin. (Hebrews 4:15)

God allows his beloved children to suffer the "natural consequences" that accompany his gift of free will. While this means that the innocent will be hurt by natural disasters and the sin of other people, it also means that we can choose how to respond to every event that comes our way. Then God can bless us for our faithfulness, obedience and perseverance.

For More Reflection

1. God is calling you! He wants to connect with you. In your journal, answer the following question: What am I ready to do in response to God's call?

2. Reflect and pray about how you can show that you are really listening to Jesus. How can you come to daily know him better?

3. Thinking about your schedule, how can you find time for more prayer and Bible study? What can you do to get more out of your times with God? (e.g., take a "prayer walk" with a friend each morning, get a new Bible, buy a devotional book, make a list of things and people you want to pray for, etc.)

4. Has someone been abusive to you in the past? If so, have you been willing to open up about it and get help in understanding and in forgiving? What does it mean to you that Jesus wants to connect with you in your hurt? That he wants to help you to move on to forgiveness?

Step 2: Allow Him to Empower You

For to be sure, he was crucified in weakness, yet he lives by God's power. Likewise, we are weak in him, yet by God's power we will live with him to serve you. (2 Corinthians 13:4)

Despite our sin, weakness and inadequacy, God wants to use each of us to accomplish his great purposes, to live a life like Jesus in this present age. In fact, Jesus promised that, thanks to his Spirit's work in our lives, we would be able to do even more than he did (John 14:12). Can we imagine being able to forgive as he forgave?

Before we look at how God can use us, though, let's talk about weakness. This word means "defect." I don't know about you, but this is not my favorite topic. Thinking about my weaknesses—my sins, character flaws, physical frailties, life challenges—makes me feel vulnerable, and this exposes my insecurity. So my preference is to talk about positive, upbeat things. But what does God prefer?

Face Our Weakness

God is crystal clear: he wants us to face our weakness, so we see our need to rely on him:

> But he said to me, "My grace is sufficient for you, for my power is made perfect in weakness." Therefore I will boast all the more gladly about my weaknesses, so that Christ's power may rest on me. That is why, for Christ's sake, I delight in weaknesses, in insults, in hardships, in persecutions, in difficulties. For when I am weak, then I am strong. (2 Corinthians 12:9–10)

> But God chose the foolish things of the world to shame the wise; God chose the weak things of the world to shame the strong. (1 Corinthians 1:27)

> And what more shall I say? I do not have time to tell about Gideon, Barak, Samson, Jephthah, David, Samuel and the prophets, who through faith conquered kingdoms, administered justice, and gained what was promised; who shut the mouths of lions, quenched the fury of the flames, and escaped the edge of the sword; whose weakness was turned to strength; and who became powerful in battle and routed foreign armies. (Hebrews 11:32–34)

This presents us with a dilemma: since we really do not know how to rely on God, what do we do? We usually pretend to be strong and capable to avoid facing the possibility (and our fear) of failure.

The title of this section is: "allow him to empower you," and yet, here we are talking about weakness. Yet it is our weakness that God can use. He wants to use the gifts, talents, resources, experiences, education and knowledge that he has given us, but he will not begin until we confront our weakness. God can only be glorified when we fully accept and acknowledge that, despite our best efforts, we cannot do anything of value without his power and intervention.

As we consider the need to forgive others, we know we need God's help. We are naturally weak in this area. Jesus is clear in stating how crucial our forgiveness of others is: if we do not forgive men their sins, our Father will not forgive us.

As I mentioned earlier, when we are hurt and mistreated, it is difficult for us to forgive others. Jesus connects with us in our hurt, and then he empowers us to forgive. Finally, he enables us to let go and allow him to be the final judge—not us. He is our ultimate example in this area:

> When they hurled their insults at him, he did not retaliate; when he suffered, he made no threats. Instead, he entrusted himself to him who judges justly. (1 Peter 2:23)

In the same way, we must entrust ourselves to him who judges justly. If those who sinned against us never repent, God will bring judgment upon them himself. It is not our place to do that. And if they do repent, they will suffer the consequences of knowing the hurt they brought to us. This will be part of their mourning process, on their way to God's forgiveness.

We must give up our need to hold on to bitterness or hatred. We must as a follower of Jesus allow his spirit to enable us to do the seemingly impossible: to forgive.

For More Reflection

1. Reflect on your God-given talents and gifts. How can God use you to accomplish his purposes? How will a forgiving spirit help accomplish God's purposes in the lives of those you forgive?

2. What weaknesses are you ready to accept and acknowledge so God can empower you in these areas?

3. Are you aware of weakness in the area of forgiving others? What are the thoughts that come to your mind when you consider forgiving those who have hurt you? Do you believe that God can empower you in this area?

4. In your journal, list three things you will do, beginning today, to live as Jesus lived. List three more things that you will do to love as he loved.

Step 3: Allow Him to Move You

> For it is God who works in you to will and to act according to his good purpose. (Philippians 2:13)

The important words in this verse are "it is God." By now we have learned that, if we are to accomplish anything worthwhile, it will not happen because of our goodness, talents or effort. It will be God's amazing power, grace and love, our awesome God who is willing to use imperfect, sinful people to achieve his great plans. He takes people who are not naturally forgiving; he frees them from their sin, and moves them to act in ways that show how they have forgiven others.

When the Lord spoke through the prophet Zechariah about the restoration of Jerusalem and the rebuilding of his temple, he said:

> "This is the word of the LORD to Zerubbabel: 'Not by might nor by power, but by my Spirit,' says the LORD Almighty." (Zechariah 4:6)

God makes and carries out his plans, and nothing can prevent him from achieving his grand design. Whether we become his instruments depends on our desire to be used and our willingness to trust him enough to sacrifice our selfish ambition and goals in order to be part of something infinitely greater. It also depends upon our willingness to be moved to forgive others so he can freely move us to accomplish the plans he has laid out for us.

Once we decide we are ready and eager to be used by God, the important question becomes, "How can I convince God to use me?" The answer is, "Ask!" Now is the time for prayer—not just a quick "head prayer," but the kind of deep, heartfelt prayer referred to by James: "The prayer of a righteous man is powerful and effective" (James 5:16b).

In *The Prayer of the Righteous,* Mark Templer describes the following "prayers of impact":[1]

- *Intimate prayer*: God listens and responds to the prayers of those who love him passionately and are completely devoted to knowing and obeying him.

- *Mighty prayer*: God wants us to fully believe that he has chosen us, and that he wants to use us. Isaiah writes:

> Then I heard the voice of the LORD saying, "Whom shall I send? And who will go for us?" And I said, "Here am I. Send me!" (Isaiah 6:8)

God always listens to our prayers, but he can be glorified when we pray for mighty works—works that can only be accomplished through him. Mighty prayers are also specific—not just asking God to "bless this day," but telling him how we need him to work. There have been many times since beginning this book that I would sit down to write with only a brief outline of what needed to come next, but after praying that God would give me the words, he did!

- *Aggressive prayer*: Some of the prayers recorded in the Bible are shocking: the petitioners are so bold and audacious, you would expect God to strike them dead for disrespect. But instead, God moves in amazing ways. Examples include Abraham's bargaining with God over the fate of Sodom (Genesis 18:23–32) and Jacob's claim that he would not let the angel go until he received a blessing (Genesis 32:24–28). This kind of bold prayer even seems presumptuous at times, such as Joshua telling the sun to stand still (Joshua 10:12–13).

- *Creative prayer*: Are you still in love with God? In Revelation 2, Jesus rebukes the church in Ephesus for forgetting their first love. What are you doing to add variety to your walk with God? Variety has been called "the spice of life" because it keeps relationships fresh.

  My husband and I often counsel married couples that being in love and staying in love requires variety, in your intimate relationship and your love for God. Here in Hawaii we have "mauka" (mountain) rain—little summer sprinkles of rain that cool us off and keep everything vibrant and green. Keeping your relationship with God creative is the mauka rain you need to remain vibrant and growing.

Inspiring Heroes of Prayer

To be able to forgive others on a daily basis and then act on their behalf, you will need a deep prayer life. If your prayer life is getting a little stale, allow the heroes of the faith to inspire you. Consider how God's heart was moved by Hannah:

> In bitterness of soul Hannah wept much and prayed to the Lord. And she made a vow, saying, "O Lord Almighty, if you will only look upon your servant's misery and remember me, and not forget your servant but give her a son, then I will give him to the Lord for all the

> days of his life, and no razor will ever be used on his head."
>
> As she kept on praying to the LORD, Eli observed her mouth. Hannah was praying in her heart, and her lips were moving but her voice was not heard. Eli thought she was drunk and said to her, "How long will you keep on getting drunk? Get rid of your wine."
>
> "Not so, my lord," Hannah replied, "I am a woman who is deeply troubled. I have not been drinking wine or beer; I was pouring out my soul to the LORD. Do not take your servant for a wicked woman; I have been praying here out of my great anguish and grief."
>
> Eli answered, "Go in peace, and may the God of Israel grant you what you have asked of him."
>
> She said, "May your servant find favor in your eyes." Then she went her way and ate something, and her face was no longer downcast. (1 Samuel 1:10–18)

Hannah felt bitter but she still called out to God. How many of us get bitter and give up on God, assuming that he will not answer anyway? Hannah "wept much," crying out to God in desperation. The passage also says "Hannah was praying in her heart." This is the kind of prayer God wants. She tells Eli, "I was pouring out my soul…out of my great anguish and grief." Crusty old Eli is even moved by her words, asking God to grant her prayer.

Finally, as Hannah went away "her face was no longer downcast." She believed that God would answer.

God responded by giving her Samuel, and after his birth Hannah again raises her voice in prayer, praising God for his goodness and mercy (1 Samuel 2:1–10).

Five chapters later, we see the Israelites asking Samuel to pray for them. Samuel responds, "Assemble all Israel at Mizpah and I will intercede with the LORD for you." The people fast and confess their sins. Then the Philistines get wind of the Israelites' meeting and decide this is a good opportunity to attack.

The Israelites again go to Samuel: "Do not stop crying out to the

Lord our God for us, that he may rescue us...." Again, Samuel "cried out to the Lord on Israel's behalf, and the Lord answered him" (1 Samuel 7:2–13).

We can guess how Samuel became such a man of prayer: although Hannah dedicated Samuel to the Lord and he grew up at the temple, in the times they did have together she probably shared with him how she had cried and pleaded for a son. They may have chuckled about how Eli even thought she was drunk.

Imagine how Hannah may have even joined with her son in prayer, praising God for his great blessings. This is how children learn to love God. Despite the importance of a church's children's ministry program, this will not lead our children to God. Instead, it is the parents who model a meaningful daily walk with him. When our children see us loving God and relying on him through every challenge, they learn that life with God is the only life that works.

Personally, I need consistent, focused prayer to overcome my selfishness—to have the heart to overflow with compassion. I must continue to allow Jesus—the living Word—to penetrate my heart and mind, and make every effort to put his word into practice. In Luke 8:15 Jesus tells the crowd

> "But the seed on good soil stands for those with a noble and good heart, who hear the word, retain it, and by persevering produce a crop."

Often we know what we should do, but we are just not motivated to do it. This "noble and good heart" Jesus refers to is our source of motivation, and it comes by studying and then obeying the Scriptures. Then we will want to be merciful and compassionate. God always rewards obedience. As we seek him to help us be compassionate and generous and forgiving, he promises

- Healing (Psalm 41:1–3)
- Security (Psalm 112:4–8)

- Respect (Proverbs 11:16)
- The ability to honor him (Proverbs 14:31)
- Guidance and satisfaction of our needs (Isaiah 58:10–11)
- His forgiveness (Matthew 6:14)
- Eternal life (Matthew 25:34, 46)

For More Reflection

1. List at least five ways God has been compassionate with you. Take some time to thank and praise him for his grace in your life.

2. As you read the example of deep prayer in the life of Hannah, how were you moved to seek God more earnestly in your life?

3. Who do you need to forgive? In what relationships are you still holding onto old hurts and resentments? Take a moment right now to apologize to God for being unforgiving, and ask him to give you the heart to fully forgive these people.

4. Since Jesus told us to pray for those who have hurt us, promise God that you will pray for those you are choosing to forgive.

❄

"...for they shall obtain mercy." Of all the Beatitudes, this one is most clearly related to our eternal destiny. Jesus promises that only when we have the heart to forgive others, will we be forgiven as well. Beyond that immeasurable reward, it is impossible to overstate the impact that the ability to forgive has on our relationships. A merciful heart is necessary to achieve unity with our family members, friends, and co-workers, and it moves us one step closer to true oneness with God, which we'll develop more fully in our next chapter.

7

Value Holiness

"Blessed are the pure in heart,
for they will see God."

Matthew 5:8

If one beatitude expresses the theme of Christ's Sermon on the Mount—in fact, his entire teaching—this is it. Against the backdrop of the Pharisees' legalism, Jesus had come to impart a refreshing message: your heart is what counts, your inner thoughts and motives are more important to God than the religious rituals you practice or traditions you keep. Most of all, Jesus decried the hypocrisy he saw—those who failed to practice what they preached, those whose worship was about empty routine rather than about genuine faith.

Nowadays people do not talk much about heart, unless they are discussing the effect of high cholesterol, the importance of aerobic exercise or the triple bypass Uncle George had last week. We tend to consider the mind the seat of personality, motivation and emotion. Likewise, although Jesus uses the word "heart," he is probably referring here to the mind, to those whose thoughts and intentions are pure. Proverbs 23:7 (NKJV) reads: "For as he thinks in his heart, so is he."

Jesus knew that thoughts tend to produce emotions—the ways we think about events (and the things we say to ourselves) have a powerful effect on the way we feel about those events. Paul advised that

> Whatever is true, whatever is noble, whatever is right, whatever is pure, whatever is lovely, whatever is admirable—if anything is excellent or praiseworthy—think about such things. Whatever you have

> learned or received or heard from me, or seen in me—put it into practice. And the God of peace will be with you. (Philippians 4:8–9)

A well-researched treatment for depression involves teaching a depressed person to think about events in a new, more constructive way, since our beliefs determine how we feel about ourselves and our lives in general. This "rational emotive" therapy is based on the work of Albert Ellis, and involves teaching a client how to identify irrational beliefs and assumptions that lead to unhealthy emotions.

Using an "A-B-C" paradigm in which *Antecedent* events lead to *Beliefs* about those events, which result in *Consequent* feelings, the idea is that if a person is able to make his beliefs more realistic (and healthy), then the emotions—the depression, anger or fear—change as well. This approach is especially helpful for people who tend to "catastrophize" (to see everything as a potential catastrophe).

Likewise, Paul teaches that if you "let God transform you into a new person by changing the way you think" (Romans 12:2, NLT), your thoughts will be based on faith, not fear, and you will generally feel more hopeful and optimistic.

Earlier we discussed the sequence of the Beatitudes, how they lead to each other in logical order. Once we see our spiritual bankruptcy and respond with wholehearted devotion, we experience and mourn the impact of our sin. This helps us grow in meekness and a readiness to surrender. When we finally long for and commit ourselves to spiritual growth, we see God's amazing mercy, which should give us the ability to be merciful with other people.

Here is where I become painfully aware of my selfish ambition, bitterness and competitive nature. Although I am incredibly grateful for God's mercy, I am still not able to imitate his heart of mercy through a sheer act of my will. Only God can transform me into someone who is naturally compassionate, forgiving and loving. I can definitely relate to Paul's complaint:

> I know that nothing good lives in me, that is, in my sinful nature. For I have the desire to do what is good, but I cannot carry it out. For what I do is not the good I want to do; no, the evil I do not want to do—this I keep on doing. (Romans 7:18–19)

Sure, I can act loving, but that is exactly what it is—an act. I suppose this is God's way of keeping us humble and helping us grow since, to move ahead, we must begin to…

Value Holiness

When we "value" something, we consider it extremely worthwhile. It is what we really want, what we are willing to work for. We are willing to sacrifice for our values, to pay a great price or give up something else that is important in exchange for what is most precious to us.

For example, Christ decided to give up his life in exchange for us so we could be with him for eternity, because we are that precious to him!

This brings us to the big question: What is the price of holiness? What will it cost us? As we discuss the following three steps, we will consider the answer to this question.

- Adopt Christlike Behavior: Because words and actions reveal the underlying heart, imitating Jesus is an essential first step toward growth in purity.
- Adopt a Godly Perspective: We must always ask whether our thinking advances or limits God's rule in our lives.
- Adopt the Zeal of Jesus: Caring about the same things that Jesus cared about, with a similar passion, is the way to grow in holy zeal.

Step 1: Adopt Christlike Behavior

> Be imitators of God, therefore, as dearly loved children and live a life of love, just as Christ loved us and gave himself up for us as a fragrant offering and sacrifice to God. (Ephesians 5:1–2)

Although Jesus is looking for a heart that is right, sometimes the only place to begin is by changing our behavior. The saying goes, "Fake it till you make it!" Yes, it may be an act at first, but the more you behave like Jesus, the more you will grow to be like him.

When the kindergarten teacher Miss Jenny is trying to teach little Suzy to raise her hand before talking in the group, she may give Suzy a gold star whenever she remembers to raise her hand. After getting ten gold stars, Suzy receives a special award and gets to sit up front with Miss Jenny for the day.

At first, Suzy will raise her hand because she likes getting the gold stars. But, after enjoying the positive attention from Miss Jenny and her classmates, eventually she will raise her hand just for these good feelings, and Miss Jenny can gradually stop giving Suzy stars. Finally, raising her hand becomes a habit, and Suzy will keep raising her hand even if she does not get any special recognition.

In the same way, asking the question, "What would Jesus do?" may seem overly religious or superficial, but it still makes sense if it helps me change my behavior while I am waiting for my heart to catch up.

God's Word Changes Hearts

The reverse is also true: the more we have the heart of Christ, the more Christlike our behavior will be. How can your heart change? Think about the following verses:

> Consequently, faith comes from hearing the message, and the message is heard through the word of Christ. (Romans 10:17)

> "Make them holy by your truth; teach them your word, which is truth." (John 17:17, NLT)
>
> There's nothing like the written Word of God for showing you the way to salvation through faith in Christ Jesus. (2 Timothy 3:15, The Message)

These and other passages make it clear that the Scriptures are able to change our hearts, to mold and purify us so we become more Christlike from the inside out. Of course this is not an overnight process. Spiritual growth is much like human development: with our cooperation, over the course of years through a series of starts, stops, mistakes and victories, God works to mature us until we become fully the person he created.

Price to Pay

This is where values come in: because we desire to be spiritually mature and useful to God, he is able to work in our lives to transform us. The price we pay for godly behavior is our willingness to sacrifice the temporary thrill of worldly pleasures (such as illicit sex or drugs); popularity with thrill-seeking peers; or the "comforts" of a selfish, easy life in order to gain something much more permanent and satisfying.

Our ultimate goal is to become completely one with Christ, so that he lives through us, as well as in us. This was the message of the Apostle Paul to the Philippians:

> But whatever was to my profit I now consider loss for the sake of Christ. What is more, I consider everything a loss compared to the surpassing greatness of knowing Christ Jesus my Lord, for whose sake I have lost all things. I consider them rubbish, that I may gain Christ and be found in him, not having a righteousness of my own that comes from the law, but that which is through faith in Christ—the righteousness that comes from God and is by faith. I want to know Christ

> and the power of his resurrection and the fellowship of sharing in his sufferings, becoming like him in his death, and so, somehow, to attain to the resurrection from the dead.
>
> Not that I have already obtained all this, or have already been made perfect, but I press on to take hold of that for which Christ Jesus took hold of me. Brothers, I do not consider myself yet to have taken hold of it. But one thing I do: Forgetting what is behind and straining toward what is ahead, I press on toward the goal to win the prize for which God has called me heavenward in Christ Jesus. (Philippians 3:7–14)

Just prior to this passage, Paul lists his stellar credentials as "a Hebrew of Hebrews" (see Philippians 3:3–6). But he says none of that matters any more—in fact, all these human achievements are like rubbish or dung compared with the value of the holiness that comes through Christ.

As we consider the values that really count, we must come to a similar realization. Although we may have been proud of our accomplishments in the past, they are totally insignificant compared to what Jesus did on the cross and what he continues to do as we live in and through him. Even if some people might be impressed by my education or the things I have done, the truth is that it all means nothing.

My faith is the only thing that is important, and even that is a gift from God (Ephesians 2:8), so I cannot take credit or boast about it. No matter how perfect my behavior, how much I mature as a Christian, how much self-discipline or effort I put out, I will never be perfectly holy. But as long as I am in relationship with God, because of the cross and his great mercy, he can make me holy.

For More Reflection

1. In what ways is your heart not like Christ's? List the things he felt passionately about that are not that important to you.

2. Turn your journal sideways and make four columns. Label them (1) Situation, (2) What Jesus did, (3) What I would do, and (4) What I will do next time. Read several chapters of Mark, filling in the columns as you go. (Later you might want to come back to this question and read more of Mark, applying the questions.)

3. Write out Galatians 2:20, John 14:20 and 1 John 3:24 on index cards. Post one on your bathroom mirror, one on your refrigerator, and one in your car or office.

Step 2: Adopt a Godly Perspective

> So I tell you this, and insist on it in the Lord, that you must no longer live as the Gentiles do, in the futility of their thinking. They are darkened in their understanding and separated from the life of God because of the ignorance that is in them due to the hardening of their hearts. Having lost all sensitivity, they have given themselves over to sensuality so as to indulge in every kind of impurity, with a continual lust for more.
>
> You, however, did not come to know Christ that way. Surely you heard of him and were taught in him in accordance with the truth that is in Jesus. You were taught, with regard to your former way of life, to put off your old self, which is being corrupted by its deceitful desires; to be made new in the attitude of your minds; and to put on the new self, created to be like God in true righteousness and holiness. (Ephesians 4:17–24)

Paul refers here to purity of mind. "Futile thinking" moves us away from God, not toward him. Although the words "fruitless" or "ineffective" come to mind when I think of futility, I discovered that the primary definition of "futile" is "hopeless." Making excuses or rationalizing the emptiness of their lives are two ways that people engage in futile thinking, and this thinking hopelessly leads them down a path where they are less likely to face their real need to rely on God.

Paul goes on to say that when we allow ourselves to become insensitive to his Spirit by hardening our hearts, we surrender to sensuality, which only drives us further away from the life of peace and joy that God intends.

Some people claim that positive thinking is the key to happiness, but in *The Power of Spiritual Thinking,* Gordon Ferguson writes:

> Biblically speaking, positive spiritual thinking has as its main goal pleasing God and serving others. Therefore, happiness is not something we seek via positive thinking; it's the by-product of being spiritual.[1]

Atheists like to encourage us to "face reality" by believing that God is a myth, but atheistic thinking is actually unrealistic (or "deceitful," as Paul calls it). To be spiritually and mentally healthy, we must begin by facing the truth about our lives. Only then, when the "diagnosis" is correct, can we find the correct "treatment" for our spiritual illness.

A Godly Perspective

What is a godly perspective? When the angel Gabriel came to Mary with the news that she would give birth, she was asked to accept the unbelievable. But, instead of refusing to believe, she asked, "How will this be, since I am a virgin?" (Luke 1:34).

Mary sought more information that would help her mind to "catch up" with her faithful heart. After explaining that the Holy Spirit would come over her so that "the holy one to be born will be called the Son of God" (Luke 1:35b), Gabriel added five simple but profound words that are the essence of spiritual thinking: "Nothing is impossible with God" (Luke 1:37).

Ask yourself: What would my life be like if I really believed that

- God is all-powerful and all-loving,
- God has chosen me, loves me and wants to bless me,
- God is right here with me now and in every moment of my life,
- God wants to use me as he used the Bible's heroes to work his miracles?

God's ability to work in our lives depends on our faith. In the following passage, Jesus tells the blind men that, because of their faith, he is restoring their sight:

> When he had gone indoors, the blind men came to him, and he asked them, "Do you believe that I am able to do this?"
>
> "Yes, Lord," they replied.
>
> Then he touched their eyes and said, "According to your faith will it be done to you"; and their sight was restored. Jesus warned them sternly, "See that no one knows about this." (Matthew 9:28–30)

The Amplified Bible translates verse 29, "According to your faith and trust and reliance [on the power invested in me] be it done to you." Jesus is not looking for passive faith or strong people who think they can go it alone; he is seeking those who, through faith, will count on his help for their lives.

On the other hand, when Jesus returned to Nazareth, his neighbors refused to believe that this man, whom they had known as a boy, could be sent from God, so he "did not do many miracles there":

> And they took offense at him. But Jesus said to them, "Only in his hometown and in his own house is a prophet without honor." And he did not do many miracles there because of their lack of faith. (Matthew 13:57–58)

Mark 6:5 reads, "he *could* not do any miracles there" (emphasis added). I do not think our unbelief actually limits God's power. But when people react to him with hostility rather than with a seeking spirit (a desire to believe), he simply refuses to act. Jesus told his followers:

> Don't waste what is holy on people who are unholy. Don't throw your pearls to pigs! They will trample the pearls, then turn and attack you. (Matthew 7:6, NLT)

Desire to Believe

The person who cannot see God working in her life must ask, "Do I even want to believe?"

Does your thinking advance God's kingdom or limit it? Peter was one of Jesus' closest companions, a man who tended to be brash and impulsive—a man many of us can relate to. He was the first disciple called by Jesus; he walked on water, and he preached the first major sermon after the resurrection. Look at the following interaction:

> When Jesus came to the region of Caesarea Philippi, he asked his disciples, "Who do people say that the Son of Man is?"
>
> "Well," they replied, "some say John the Baptist, some say Elijah, and others say Jeremiah or one of the other prophets."
>
> Then he asked them, "But who do you say I am?"
>
> Simon Peter answered, "You are the Messiah, the Son of the living God."
>
> Jesus replied, "You are blessed, Simon son of John, because my Father in heaven has revealed this to you. You did not learn this from any human being. Now I say to you that you are Peter (which means 'rock'), and upon this rock I will build my church, and all the powers of hell will not conquer it. And I will give you the keys of the Kingdom of Heaven. Whatever you forbid on earth will be forbidden in heaven, and whatever you permit on earth will be permitted in heaven." (Matthew 16:13–19, NLT)

Wow! Peter must have felt incredible, and maybe a little prideful at being singled out by Jesus. But let us read on:

> Then he sternly warned the disciples not to tell anyone that he was the Messiah. From then on Jesus began to tell his disciples plainly that it was necessary for him to go to Jerusalem, and that he would suffer many terrible things at the hands of the elders, the leading priests, and the teachers of religious law. He would be killed, but on the third day he would be raised from the dead.
>
> But Peter took him aside and began to reprimand him for saying such things. "Heaven forbid, Lord," he said. "This will never happen to you!"
>
> Jesus turned to Peter and said, "Get away from me, Satan! You are a dangerous trap to me. You are seeing things merely from a human point of view, not from God's." (Matthew 16:20–23, NLT)

Whoops—just when Peter was feeling great about himself, he allowed worldliness to creep in. Feeling stung by Jesus' words, he may have thought, "Jesus, I was only trying to protect you!" But Jesus had a heavenly agenda, not a worldly one.

Growing in Godliness

How can you adopt a more godly perspective? Try the following suggestions:

- Watch out for ungodly influences.

> Blessed (happy, fortunate, prosperous and enviable) is the man who walks and lives not in the counsel of the ungodly [following their advice, their plans and purposes], nor stands [submissive and inactive] in the path where sinners walk, nor sits down [to relax and rest] where the scornful [and the mockers] gather. (Psalm 1:1, Amplified)

- Love the Scriptures and memorize passages that build your faith.

> But his delight and desire are in the law of the Lord, and on His law (the precepts, the instructions, the teachings of God) he habitually

meditates (ponders and studies) by day and by night. (Psalm 1:2, Amplified)

- Study the teaching of Jesus, paying attention to the ways his perspective differs from his contemporaries and your own thinking. (Chapters 5 through 7 of Matthew are a great place to begin this study.)

For, "Who can know the Lord's thoughts? Who knows enough to teach him?" But we understand these things, for we have the mind of Christ. (1 Corinthians 2:16, NLT)

- Beware of pessimism. Instead, ask what God could be doing to create good from the situation.

To the pure, all things are pure, but to those who are corrupted and do not believe, nothing is pure. In fact, both their minds and consciences are corrupted. (Titus 1:15)

For More Reflection

1. Read the following scriptures and answer the question for each passage:
   - A. John 2:13–17: Why did Jesus react so strongly? Would you have this kind of outrage?
   - B. Matthew 26:36–46: How did Jesus react to his friends when they fell asleep at his most difficult time? How would you react?
   - C. Luke 23:32–34: What motivated Jesus to pray for the people who tortured and killed him? What would you do in this situation?

2. Are you eager to spend time in the Word each day? Would you rather go without food than without a day in the Scriptures? How long has it been since your Bible study helped you resist a specific temptation?

3. Write a plan for putting into practice each of the above four suggestions for adopting a godly perspective.

Step 3: Adopt the Zeal of Jesus

He put on righteousness as his breastplate,
and the helmet of salvation on his head;
he put on the garments of vengeance
and wrapped himself in zeal as in a cloak. (Isaiah 59:17)

Jesus was full of zeal for the things of God. Zeal is enthusiasm, devotion, fervor, intensity or passion. To be zealous is not just to feel strongly but to take radical action, action that may look to others like evidence of insanity. Even Jesus' mother and brothers thought he was crazy (Mark 3:20–21).

To be zealous is to risk being ridiculed, rejected and abandoned—all the things we fear but Jesus experienced because he burned with an intensity that shocked and frightened even the twelve. To imitate him and enjoy his life to the full, we must first understand what he was zealous about, and then how he expressed that zeal.

What were the things that lit a fire in Jesus? (Many of the following passages refer to God, but these would clearly be characteristics of Jesus as well.)

1. Sin and Righteousness

Throughout the Old and New Testaments, God urges his people to repent of sin and pursue righteousness. God wants us to follow his teachings not because he is a "cosmic killjoy" but for our own good (Deuteronomy 6:24). Jesus was hated by the religious establishment because he was radical on sin, emphasizing purity of thoughts, motives and intentions—not just external obedience.

> You love righteousness and hate wickedness;
> therefore God, your God, has set you above your companions
> by anointing you with the oil of joy. (Psalm 45:7)

> And if your eye causes you to sin, gouge it out and throw it away. It is better for you to enter life with one eye than to have two eyes and be thrown into the fire of hell. (Matthew 18:9)

2. Oppression, Poverty and Injustice

The fact that there are more than 100 Biblical references to *oppression* and 100+ references to *justice* underscores their importance to God. Throughout history, oppression, poverty and injustice have been intimately related. The poor are oppressed by slave owners, landowners, kings and employers—the rich and powerful. According to Thomas Hanks' book, *God So Loved the Third World* there are a variety of Hebrew roots for the word "oppression" which are translated as crush, humiliate, animalize, impoverish, enslave and kill.[2] These words describe the experience of the Israelites—and other oppressed groups—throughout history.

According to Lowell Noble, "We should probably regard *daka* as the strongest Hebrew word denoting oppression.... [It] occurs 31 times...10 times with the poor. Oppression smashes the body and crushes the human spirit. That is, God's image is pulverized like a moth crushed under a boot heel."[3]

How does God feel about oppression?

> Woe to those who make unjust laws, to those who issue oppressive decrees, to deprive the poor of their rights and withhold justice from the oppressed of my people, making widows their prey and robbing the fatherless. (Isaiah 10:1–2)

3. God's Honor and His Name

In Malachi 1:6 God asks the question, "If I am a father, where is the honor due me?" Although God commands us to honor our fathers, he wants us to honor him not out of duty but love. God meets all our needs. He gives us life and then he showers our lives with blessing.

When we are ill, facing financial hardship or feeling worried or fearful about the future, it is more difficult to be grateful. But under all circumstances God is there, loving us unconditionally, ready to encourage and help us if we will only trust and rely on him. In return, he expects our best—our best sacrifice, our greatest reverence and our most heartfelt worship.

Through the prophet Malachi, God tells the people that he is not pleased when they give him their leftovers. In modern times we may not sacrifice animals, but we offer him our lives. Paul told the Romans: "Offer your bodies as living sacrifices, holy and pleasing to God—this is your spiritual act of worship" (Romans 12:1).

Just as Malachi urged the people to offer God undefiled sacrifices, which foreshadowed Christ as the unblemished Lamb of God, our lives must be holy if we are to please our loving Father.

Honoring God also means revering him and holding his name in the highest regard. When we idly stand by and permit people to casually use God's name or, worse, to turn it into a curse, we dishonor and displease the One who has provided everything that is good.

Finally, honoring God means worshipping him "in spirit and truth" (John 4:23). Wholehearted worship is not about what we get out of it—being entertained, feeling good or getting our weekly "injection of spirituality." It is about giving God the glory and honor he deserves.

Our love affair with big-scale entertainment has fooled us into believing that glitz is necessary for meaningful worship, but the opposite is true: the more simplicity, the more we can focus on God rather than on a spectacular human performance. A related issue is the preaching: when someone complains that they do not look forward to going to church because a particular person is giving the message, they miss the whole point.

How does God feel about all this? Consider the following passage:

> Phinehas son of Eleazar, the son of Aaron, the priest, has turned my anger away from the Israelites; for he was as zealous as I am for my honor among them, so that in my zeal I did not put an end to them. Therefore tell him I am making my covenant of peace with him. (Numbers 25:11–12)

One person's zeal changed God's mind about destroying the Israelites! Would you have been that person?

4. Hypocrisy and Heartless Ritual

The title of this section could be, "Tell the truth." In Matthew 23, Jesus condemns the Pharisees not for their teaching but for their lives. This is also a problem today. How many of us really practice the things we say we believe, such as reaching out to a lost world, feeding the hungry or continuing to love those who are hateful or unrepentant?

Hypocrisy is detestable to God because it is based on deceit. The hypocrite is an actor, playing the role of a person who trusts in God while actually worshipping the idols of self, other people or material things.

Religious ritual is one form of hypocrisy. Our worship means nothing if it is not accompanied by sincere humility before God, a recognition that we do not measure up to his standard, so we can never look down on non-Christians or those who continue to sin openly, despite professing to follow Jesus. It is sad but true that much of today's "Christianity" is simply human religion in the name of Jesus.

Rather than a transformation into servants who are devoted to

Christ's mission, our Christianity can be simply a veneer of righteousness that conceals an unrighteous character. This hypocrisy is guaranteed to turn off many of those who desperately need God's grace.

5. Respect for God's House

> No one who practices deceit
> will dwell in my house;
> no one who speaks falsely
> will stand in my presence. (Psalm 101:7)

In the Old Testament we see the importance of God's house, his temple, to the Israelites' worship. David writes:

> One thing I ask of the LORD,
> this is what I seek:
> that I may dwell in the house of the LORD
> all the days of my life,
> to gaze upon the beauty of the LORD
> and to seek him in his temple. (Psalm 27:4)

Then, when Jesus clears the temple (see John 2), his disciples remember these words of David:

> I am a stranger to my brothers,
> an alien to my own mother's sons;
> for zeal for your house consumes me,
> and the insults of those who insult you fall on me. (Psalm 69:8–9)

In fact, David had wanted to build the temple, but God gave David's son, Solomon, this great honor. The first nine chapters of 2 Chronicles, in particular, center on the temple. Solomon's prayer at the dedication of the new temple includes these words:

> "But will God really dwell on earth with men? The heavens, even the highest heavens, cannot contain you. How much less this temple I have built! Yet give attention to your servant's prayer and his plea for

> mercy, O LORD my God. Hear the cry and the prayer that your servant is praying in your presence. May your eyes be open toward this temple day and night, this place of which you said you would put your Name there. May you hear the prayer your servant prays toward this place. Hear the supplications of your servant and of your people Israel when they pray toward this place. Hear from heaven, your dwelling place; and when you hear, forgive." (2 Chronicles 6:18–21)

Why was the temple so significant? Because it was the place where the people would find answered prayer and blessing. Now, with the advent of Christianity, God's Spirit no longer resides in a physical building but in us as believers, since we ourselves are temples of the living God. Paul tells the Corinthians:

> Do you not know that your body is a temple of the Holy Spirit, who is in you, whom you have received from God? You are not your own; you were bought at a price. Therefore honor God with your body. (1 Corinthians 6:19–20)

Consider the tremendous implication of these words. First, how could we possibly suffer from low self-worth when we are the Lord's temple? Also, when we abuse our bodies through overindulgence, lack of sleep or inactivity, we are defiling the temple of God.

Finally, just as an Israelite would be blessed by coming to the temple and surrendering to God, we must allow Christ to be King of our lives so that he can build us as a church "into a spiritual house to be a holy priesthood, offering spiritual sacrifices acceptable to God" (1 Peter 2:5). That brings us to the topic of the church.

6. The Church, God's People

The following passage communicates the heart of Christ for his church, and especially his passionate desire to protect and maintain her holiness:

> Don't you know that you yourselves are God's temple and that God's Spirit lives in you? If anyone destroys God's temple, God will destroy him; for God's temple is sacred, and you are that temple. (1 Corinthians 3:16–17)

Christ's church is composed of people who are fully devoted to God as Lord and King. Paul writes to the Ephesians:

> And God placed all things under his feet and appointed him to be head over everything for the church, which is his body, the fullness of him who fills everything in every way. (Ephesians 1:22–23)

We are the power of Christ in this world. We are the fullness of his body, his treasured possession, and the vehicle for doing his work—preaching good news to the poor, proclaiming freedom for the prisoners and recovery of sight for the blind, releasing the oppressed (Luke 4:18).

Of the marital relationship, which mirrors Christ's relationship with the church, Paul says, "Husbands, love your wives, just as Christ loved the church and gave himself up for her" (Ephesians 5:25). No wonder Christ is so zealous about his church: he suffered and died to save her!

Another important question is how we become part of God's church. At Pentecost, with Peter preaching his first major sermon after the resurrection, the writer of Acts tells us:

> Peter replied, "Each of you must repent of your sins and turn to God, and be baptized in the name of Jesus Christ for the forgiveness of your sins. Then you will receive the gift of the Holy Spirit. This promise is to you, and to your children, and even to the Gentiles—all who have been called by the Lord our God."
>
> Then Peter continued preaching for a long time, strongly urging all his listeners, "Save yourselves from this crooked generation!" Those who believed what Peter said were baptized and added to the church that day—about 3,000 in all. (Acts 2:38–41 NLT)

Peter preached that through repentance and baptism they would receive forgiveness and the gift of the Spirit. That response also brought them into God's church—the body of Christ (1 Corinthians 12:13). Declaring that "Jesus is Lord" and surrendering our lives in baptism, our sinful nature is buried with him. Then, we are raised to live a new life under his reign and in his power (Romans 6:4), and do it in fellowship with others.

It is essential that this not be merely a "theology," but instead a practicality—that we actually *live* under the control of Christ more and more from that day forward. True, we will repeatedly sin by trying to retake control of our own lives, but repentance always brings refreshment and renewed purpose (Acts 3:19). As his people, we must bear in mind that the resurrected Christ can live and work in our world only to the extent that we are surrendered to his reign, filled with and empowered by his Spirit.

It is sad that some say they love God but would rather not be part of a church. Perhaps it is because we are poor representatives of our Lord. It may be that these folks have been hurt by other Christians so they are disenchanted with the whole idea of "church." Of course, each of us is imperfect—sinful—so we will continue to hurt and be hurt by each other (and will be called to forgive over and over again). Despite all this, God's plan is still flawless. If we remain humble in our weakness and trust him, he will continue to use us to fulfill that perfect plan.

7. Idolatry and Rebellion

There are few more moving sermons than Stephen's speech before the Sanhedrin (Acts 7). In it, Stephen presents the history of the Jewish nation from Abraham to Solomon. What is striking is how often, despite all the ways God blessed them, the rebellious Israelites would turn away from him to worship idols, and how God continued to be merciful instead of treating them as they deserved, by annihilating them from the earth.

Toward the end of his message, Stephen sums up their history and, at the same time, seals his own fate with the following words:

> "You stubborn people! You are heathen at heart and deaf to the truth. Must you forever resist the Holy Spirit? That's what your ancestors did, and so do you! Name one prophet your ancestors didn't persecute! They even killed the ones who predicted the coming of the Righteous One—the Messiah whom you betrayed and murdered. You deliberately disobeyed God's law, even though you received it from the hands of angels." (Acts 7:51–53, NLT)

We can be tempted to think that, because God does not squash us like a bug, he does not see or feel strongly about our rebellion. But it is simply God's love that keeps us safe. What he said about his people Israel is still applicable to us as the new Israel:

> For you are a holy people, who belong to the LORD your God. Of all the people on earth, the LORD your God has chosen you to be his own special treasure.
>
> The LORD did not set his heart on you and choose you because you were more numerous than other nations, for you were the smallest of all nations! Rather, it was simply that the LORD loves you, and he was keeping the oath he had sworn to your ancestors. That is why the LORD rescued you with such a strong hand from your slavery and from the oppressive hand of Pharaoh, king of Egypt. Understand, therefore, that the LORD your God is indeed God. He is the faithful God who keeps his covenant for a thousand generations and lavishes his unfailing love on those who love him and obey his commands. But he does not hesitate to punish and destroy those who reject him. Therefore, you must obey all these commands, decrees, and regulations I am giving you today. (Deuteronomy 7:6–11, NLT)

After realizing the deep love that God had for his people, we can be shocked at the Israelites' lapse into idolatry. However, we must realize that we are as prone to "worship" idols like comfort, money, material things, prestige or our own achievements. As discussed in an earlier chapter, anything we place ahead of our relationship with God qualifies as an idol in our lives.

Being Like Jesus

After seeing how God expressed his zeal, knowing that Jesus and his Father are one, we have seen the zealous heart of Jesus. In reading the Gospels, we see Jesus expressing his zeal while in the flesh on this earth. Through bold action, regardless of the consequences, Jesus continued to be loving, but at the same time he did not hesitate to speak out on behalf of the poor and oppressed or to defend God's honor. He also did not hesitate to point out sin, often quoting scripture.

Does this describe you? Are you too faithless or fearful to be like Jesus?

Many of us simply don't think of ourselves as risk-takers. Psychologists emphasize different personality traits, or underlying individual characteristics, in understanding why some people love taking risks, while others would never consider it.

Although there is disagreement even among professionals as to why some people seek thrills, we do know that a perception of risk triggers a variety of physical changes that usually accompany excitement or fear. These include trembling, nausea, diarrhea, shortness of breath, muscle tension and increased heartbeat. Since these symptoms can be very unpleasant, they help to explain why most of us are motivated to avoid risks!

But what of those who enjoy skydiving or mountain-climbing—or even who risk disapproval, humiliation and rejection? In the past, psychoanalysts believed that safety is a basic human need, so thrill-seeking must be evidence of insanity. But modern psychologists have found that risk-takers tend to be higher in a particular personality trait called "Sensation Seeking."

This may help to explain why some people seek thrills, but it is a historical fact that, regardless of personality, Christians throughout the ages have been willing to follow Jesus "out on a limb." An article that appeared in the November-December '02 issue of *Today's Christian Woman*, told the story of how two young women were imprisoned for following Jesus:

> That girl-next-door image has been reinforced by countless media stories. Yet as the women reflect on the 105 days they spent in the custody of the Taliban in Afghanistan for sharing their Christian faith, a more complex picture emerges. It becomes apparent their troubled pasts led each into a life-changing relationship with Jesus—and to the kind of risk-taking faith that motivated them to serve the "poorest of the poor" in Afghanistan with the relief agency Shelter Germany.
>
> While Heather seriously questioned God during captivity and readily admits "prison was devastatingly hard," she and Dayna still wrote and sang praise songs amidst the mice and filth to the God they'd already seen perform miracles in Afghanistan, to the God they hoped would perform just one more on their behalf.[4]

What an inspirational story! I am so grateful that God allowed these two women to live and to share their story with us. We may ask, "How can we grow to have this kind of courageous passion for the Christian faith?"

Notice that each of the three action steps in this chapter use the word "adopt." An adopted child is not a "natural" child but still grows to be as much a part of the family as a child actually born into that bloodline. God has adopted us (Ephesians 1:5), and when we adopt or "take on" the behavior, perspective and zeal of Christ, eventually we will grow to be more naturally like him in character, in our intentions, and in our ability to live in a way that pleases him.

For More Reflection

1. Following are six areas where we are commanded to "make every effort." Rate, on a one to ten scale (with one being "not at all" and ten being "totally"), how much effort you are putting into each of the following areas:

   - Make every effort to enter through the narrow door (Luke 13:24).
   - Make every effort to do what leads to peace and mutual edification (Romans 14:19).
   - Make every effort to keep the unity of the Spirit (Ephesians 4:3).
   - Make every effort to enter that rest [by obeying God] (Hebrews 4:11).
   - Make every effort to add to your faith goodness...knowledge...self-control...perseverance...godliness...brotherly kindness...love (2 Peter 1:5).
   - Make every effort to be found spotless, blameless, and at peace with him (2 Peter 3:14).

2. Consider how strongly you show zeal in each of the seven areas discussed on pages 133–140. Reflect in your journal about what changes you will need to make in your life as you begin to adopt—and express—the zeal of Jesus in these areas.

3. Do you find yourself rebelling against some of God's commands? Make a plan to change the top two areas where you are tempted to (or actually do) rebel.

In this fifth beatitude, Jesus says that the pure in heart "will see God." Perhaps this means we will be in heaven with him for eternity. Also, the more we share his heart and perspective, the more clearly we will understand, adopt and "see" God's character. This will be essential as we move to the next beatitude and begin to spread the peace of Christ.

8

Peacemaking

Encourage Reconciliation

> "Blessed are the peacemakers,
> for they will be called sons of God."
>
> Matthew 5:9

I have always considered myself a peacemaker. I hate conflict and will do just about anything to prevent it. If I think someone is angry with me, I feel a little ill in the pit of my stomach, and my natural tendency is to avoid that person. And, when other people disagree or argue, I feel somehow responsible for trying to smooth things over as quickly as possible.

That is not what Jesus meant by these words, and it is not even like Jesus. Jesus was definitely not a conflict-avoider. He was constantly at odds with the religious establishment. He loved everyone but he spoke the truth, which often insulted them and sent them off plotting ways to get revenge.

Jesus was on God's mission and he would not be stopped. When warned that his life was in danger, he did not slink away in fear, but responded confidently:

> At that time some Pharisees came to Jesus and said to him, "Leave this place and go somewhere else. Herod wants to kill you." He replied, "Go tell that fox, 'I will drive out demons and heal people today and tomorrow, and on the third day I will reach my goal.' In any case, I must keep going today and tomorrow and the next day—for surely no prophet can die outside Jerusalem!" (Luke 13:31–33)

No, Jesus was not at all timid. So exactly what kind of peacemaking results in blessing—and even being called God's child? I believe that Jesus is urging his disciples to...

Encourage Reconciliation

God calls us to encourage two types of reconciliation. The first involves reconciling people with God. In Paul's second letter to the Corinthian church, he writes:

> Since, then, we know what it is to fear the Lord, we try to persuade men....
>
> So from now on we regard no one from a worldly point of view. Though we once regarded Christ in this way, we do so no longer. Therefore, if anyone is in Christ, he is a new creation; the old has gone, the new has come! All this is from God, who reconciled us to himself through Christ and gave us the ministry of reconciliation: that God was reconciling the world to himself in Christ, not counting men's sins against them. And he has committed to us the message of reconciliation. We are therefore Christ's ambassadors, as though God were making his appeal through us. We implore you on Christ's behalf: Be reconciled to God. God made him who had no sin to be sin for us, so that in him we might become the righteousness of God. (2 Corinthians 5:11, 16–21)

Paul says that not only has he become a "new creation" since being reconciled to God, but God has given him a ministry—to persuade others to be reconciled as well. As disciples of Christ, each of us has been appointed an ambassador, reaching out to those who desperately need God's healing power in their lives.

There is nothing like the thrill of showing someone scriptures about God's love and his plan, and how he has personally called each of us to find the "life to the full" that only Christ can provide. And there is nothing like seeing that person repent in miraculous ways and finally become a baptized disciple of Jesus.

During a recent trip to San Jose to visit our kids, my son Greg said, "Mom, I know you're writing a book about joy, and I was thinking about what gives me the most joy. It's definitely helping people become Christians!" Greg inspires me to fully embrace my role of ambassador. Of all the people I know, he is the most passionate about sharing his faith. I have little doubt that Greg has studied the Bible with several hundred people, and many of them have ended up in the water of baptism. Although some of us enjoy working in the "helping professions," what an incredible experience for any of us to know that we have helped someone spend eternity with God!

God also wants us to help people reconcile with each other, particularly in our churches. Since God is love (1 John 4:8), as his people and emissaries to the world, we should be known for our unity. Jesus suggested that our ability to reconcile with each other will strongly influence the success of our mission: "By this all men will know that you are my disciples, if you love one another" (John 13:35).

Unfortunately, harmonious relationships were not easily achieved in the early church, and this is still the case today. In fact, the church in Corinth was fraught with divisions, and unity was the theme of much of Paul's teaching there:

> I appeal to you, brothers, in the name of our Lord Jesus Christ, that all of you agree with one another so that there may be no divisions among you and that you may be perfectly united in mind and thought. (1 Corinthians 1:10)

How can we encourage others to follow the Prince of Peace if there is no peace in our fellowship? The world is looking for internal peace, but have you noticed how easily this peace is disturbed by external conflict? I love Paul's advice to the Colossians:

> Let the peace of Christ rule in your hearts, since as members of one body you were called to peace. And be thankful. Let the word of Christ

> dwell in you richly as you teach and admonish one another with all wisdom, and as you sing psalms, hymns and spiritual songs with gratitude in your hearts to God. (Colossians 3:15–16)

I read somewhere that, when my heart is not at peace, that is a good sign that I am not dealing with some sin in my life. Think about it: what is the fruit of God's Spirit? Love, joy, peace, patience, kindness, goodness, gentleness, faithfulness and self-control (Galatians 5:22–23). When I am allowing his Spirit to control me, won't I be at peace internally and with my brothers and sisters in the faith?

Once again, we can put this beatitude into practice only after we have fully embraced the previous verses. By recognizing how desperately we need God's mercy and by mourning our sin, we can then surrender completely and make a commitment to spiritual growth. Then God will fill us with his compassion and righteousness, enabling us to be peacemakers who reconcile people with him and with each other.

Isn't it amazing that God has chosen to use us in this way? In fact, our ability to be a minister of reconciliation begins with gratitude:

- Appreciate His Peace: Only as disciples can we sail peacefully through life's storms with God as our anchor and the Bible our compass.
- Appreciate Your Commission: Sincerely valuing the life we have in Christ spurs us on to encourage others to be reconciled first to God, and then to each other.
- Appreciate the Challenges: Surrendering to Jesus' lordship gives us the assurance of God's help whatever hardship we face as we share his amazing message.

Being with Jesus brings us peace that can be found in no other place or no other person. He is indeed the Prince of Peace.

Step 1: Appreciate His Peace

> The fruit of righteousness will be peace; the effect of righteousness will be quietness and confidence forever. My people will live in peaceful dwelling places, in secure homes, in undisturbed places of rest. (Isaiah 32:17–18)

Peace of mind is the greatest and most sought after gift. During my years as a therapist I worked with many clients whose internal stress and anxiety were overwhelming. They spent many dollars and countless hours searching for peace of mind, but as disciples of Jesus it is ours free of charge.

Various therapeutic techniques help people prevent and cope with anxiety. These include progressive relaxation, making positive self-statements, goal-setting to increase personal control, and even the use of anti-anxiety medications. But, from my experience and reports of clients and friends, I truly believe that only a personal relationship with God can provide an inner "anchor." This anchor involves a certainty that he is in control and that, even when circumstances are grim, the final resolution will be positive. After all, the worst (or best) that can happen for a Christian is death, and then we anticipate eternity with Christ! Jesus even promised us peace:

> Peace I leave with you; my peace I give you. I do not give to you as the world gives. Do not let your hearts be troubled and do not be afraid. (John 14:27)

Unfortunately, though, many good-hearted Christians have never discovered the spiritual keys to inner peace, so they struggle with daily anxiety that prevents them from living a life of joy. Here are five fundamentals that can make the difference between stressful worry and enjoying the peace that Jesus intended:

- Forgiveness
- Acceptance
- Imitation
- Thanksgiving
- Help

Forgiveness means letting go of hurts, resentments and bitterness. It means letting God be the judge when we are abused or treated unfairly, following the advice found in this wise old saying: "Let go and let God." Forgiveness also involves the humility that comes with appreciating how much we have been forgiven and how much we still need forgiveness each day.

Acceptance means nonresistance (or "meekness" as discussed in chapter 4). It is about letting God be God so we no longer have to control life, but can just enjoy living it! Rather than fighting difficult circumstances, we can make the "Serenity Prayer" our motto:

> God grant me the serenity to accept the things I cannot change, courage to change the things I can, and wisdom to know the difference.

Imitation means learning what worked for the spiritual heroes of the Bible and imitating their example. I can imitate the faith of Abraham, the integrity of Joseph, the loyalty of Ruth, the worship of David, the wisdom of Abigail, the childlike heart of Peter, the courage of Paul. Most of all, I can imitate Jesus' unquestioning obedience and dependence on his Father, God. I find that the more I know the Scriptures and am able to put them into practice, the less guilt and insecurity I experience and the more spiritual strength I have when the challenges come. As Paul said:

> Whatever you have learned or received or heard from me, or seen in me—put it into practice. And the God of peace will be with you. (Philippians 4:9)

Thanksgiving means having a heart full of gratitude for God's word, his love, grace, forgiveness, encouragement, guidance, inspiration, comfort, protection, availability, answered prayer, patience, gifts.... I cannot imagine what life would be like without God.

Reflecting on all God continues to do for us, his children, it strikes me that he actually provides the kind of "healing climate" needed by people who seek counseling. As I grew to understand how to help various clients, I discovered that, regardless of what brought them into therapy, in order to heal and grow they needed security (feeling cared for and protected), connection (being understood), and accountability (believing that life is meaningful and we can make a difference). Essentially, when people live or work in this kind of environment, they are able to flourish and fully use their gifts.

Finally, notice how these three needs are similar to the enduring faith, love and hope that Paul mentions in his "love chapter" (1 Corinthians 13:13), and how God meets them in order to bless us!

Help means being real and open with spiritual friends who can provide comfort, prayer and biblical advice. It takes at least one special "faith partner" who can encourage you through the challenges and urge you to become fully the person God created. Most of all, "help" means going to God with everything. I love that old hymn:

> What a friend we have in Jesus,
> all our sins and griefs to bear.
> What a privilege to carry
> everything to God in prayer.
> Oh, what peace we often forfeit.
> Oh, what needless pain we bear.
> All because we do not carry
> everything to God in prayer.

You may not have noticed that our five spiritual keys spell "faith." (Some people think acronyms are hokey but they are still great memory devices!) The more faith we have, the more we will be able to trust and rely on God instead of our own resources. The more we pray, the more we will be able to practice the above fundamentals. Bible study is the primary way we build our faith (Romans 10:17).

In her book, *Calm My Anxious Heart,* Linda Dillow says, "As I think about true faith, heartfelt throw-yourself-in-with-complete-abandon faith, two things come to mind:

- Faith is rooted in God's character.
- Faith is based on God's word, not on our feelings."[1]

It is not that I am so trusting—it is that God is so trustworthy! God is sovereign and all-powerful, and God loves and wants the best for me!

When I am struggling to believe, I can go to the Bible itself which, after all, was not the creation of some man but of God himself (2 Peter 1:20–21). In the pages of Scripture I find the truth—that God is always there just waiting for me to call on him, wanting to help me with absolutely everything, from the tiniest doubt to the most gargantuan mess.

For More Reflection

1. Reflect on the five fundamentals for experiencing the peace of Christ. Answer this question in your journal: In what ways can I grow to experience greater peace in each of these areas?

2. In your journal, write about a time when you were not letting the peace of Christ rule in your heart (Colossians 3:15). What were you thinking or feeling? What can you do differently the next time you feel that way?

3. Think of a friend who needs God's peace. What scriptures can you share with her, and what spiritual advice can you give her?

Step 2: Appreciate Your Commission

> But thanks be to God, who always leads us in triumphal procession in Christ and through us spreads everywhere the fragrance of the knowledge of him. For we are to God the aroma of Christ among those who are being saved and those who are perishing. To the one we are the smell of death; to the other, the fragrance of life. And who is equal to such a task? (2 Corinthians 2:14–16)

The aroma of Christ. How can anyone deny that the Bible is God's inspired word with language like this? I wonder, what do I "smell like" to non-Christians? Sometimes I am odorless since I am keeping God's message to myself. If I allow my sinful nature to take over, then to those with open hearts, I am not fragrant, and to those with closed hearts, I am not "stinky."

I am reminded of Durian fruit, about which Wikipedia says, "The edible flesh emits a distinctive odour, strong and penetrating even when the husk is intact. Regarded by some as fragrant, others as overpowering and offensive, the smell evokes reactions from deep appreciation to intense disgust." What will it take for me to be like this fruit—stinky to those who are "closed," while at the same time smelling sweet to those who are "open"?

God's Leadership

Let us not get sidetracked and miss what Paul is saying, though. Foremost, his words reveal a profound gratitude for God's leadership, the victorious life in Christ, and the unbelievable privilege of being used to spread the knowledge of God.

Is God's leadership evident in your life? What does it mean to let God lead? As our Shepherd (Psalm 23 and John 10:1–18), God goes ahead of us. We are then to follow in his footsteps, trusting that his way leads to safety and blessing. He also protects us. Jesus called himself "the good shepherd," explaining that he knows each of us personally and even calls us by name, sacrifices his very life for us, and as long as we stay close to him, will never abandon us to "the wolf" (Satan).

Clearly, though, God will not lead us if we refuse to follow and rely on him. The Bible is replete with examples of the dangers of self-reliance and relying on men:

> At that time Hanani the seer came to Asa king of Judah and said to him: "Because you relied on the king of Aram and not on the LORD your God, the army of the king of Aram has escaped from your hand. Were not the Cushites and Libyans a mighty army with great numbers of chariots and horsemen? Yet when you relied on the LORD, he delivered them into your hand. For the eyes of the LORD range throughout the earth to strengthen those whose hearts are fully committed to him. You have done a foolish thing, and from now on you will be at war." (2 Chronicles 16:7–9)

Sadly, King Asa never learned his lesson. Resenting this advice, he imprisoned Hanani. Later he developed a severe foot disease, but still chose to rely on the physicians rather than on God, possibly resulting in his death two years later.

Expressing Gratitude

Paul also expressed his gratitude for the victories he had seen. The New Life version translates 2 Corinthians 2:14 as "He…makes us win in everything." That does not mean we will never make mistakes or experience rejection, financial hardship or even difficult relationships with Christian brothers and sisters. Winning with God means that, even when these challenges happen, we can continue to rely on God and know that he can use the struggle to increase our faith and strength of character.

Finally, Paul expressed his gratitude for the way God used him to spread the word of Christ. Because of my cowardice and unbelief, at times I can view evangelism as a burden. But the letters of Paul make it clear that each day he celebrated the great privilege of being God's messenger. In fact, his "self-worth" depended on fulfilling his mission:

> But my life is worth nothing to me unless I use it for finishing the work assigned me by the Lord Jesus—the work of telling others the Good News about the wonderful grace of God. (Acts 20:24, NLT)

It is this gratitude that compels all those who risk their reputation or their lives to tell people about Jesus. When we really appreciate the wonderful life and peace of mind that are ours in Christ, we will want to share it. And this can spur us on to encourage everyone, first, to be reconciled with God, and then with each other.

How to Motivate People

But how can we motivate people to *want* to study the Bible? A lesson I learned, first as a graduate student, and then in private practice, was that the most effective motivator for doing anything challenging is to visualize a positive result, and then imagine (or *feel*) the great feelings associated with that result.

A less effective motivator, rather than this desire to move forward, is the desire to escape something painful. The problem with escape motivation? It only takes us into our "comfort zone": once there, the motivation ends. In other words, being motivated by the need to get away from something doesn't help us continue growing so that God can truly use us for his great work.

Hebrews 12:2 tells us that Jesus endured the cross "for the joy set before him." He knew the pain he was facing, but he also knew his future reward. The question is, "How can we help people imagine and *feel* the peace and joy that a relationship with Christ will bring?" Only when we're experiencing it ourselves will we be able to express it to other people, thus giving them a desire to enjoy knowing Christ too.

However, keep in mind that Jesus experienced tremendous resistance from the religious people of his day, and this has not changed. I have found that religious people with a nominal faith can be the most difficult to persuade because they believe they are fine and because they are probably not committing what most would consider the worst sins (murder, theft). I can relate to these folks: although for many years I *wanted* a deep relationship with Christ, I did not experience my need, so I too was lulled into a false sense of security.

For More Reflection

1. Have you really accepted your commission? Are you following Matthew 28:19–20: making disciples, baptizing them, and then teaching them to live like Jesus? If you need to grow in this area, don't go it alone! Find a Christian friend who might be willing to partner with you in reconciling people with God. If you know someone who needs to reconcile with God, what can you say to encourage her to learn more about God's word and his plan for her life?

2. Read Matthew 5:23–24 and Matthew 18:15–35. Is there someone you need to reconcile with? What will you do to reach out to him or her?

3. On a scale of one to ten, what's your motivation to share the Good News? Does your gratitude for everything God provides overflow so that you *can't* keep quiet?

Step 3:
Appreciate the Challenges

The apostles left the high council rejoicing that God had counted them worthy to suffer disgrace for the name of Jesus. (Acts 5:41, NLT)

Few of us would choose to suffer (unless we have masochistic tendencies). That is why the reaction of the apostles in this verse may be foreign to our experience. We can almost wonder if the apostles began their day with the thought: "Today I'll go out and suffer for Jesus!"

Although the apostles rejoiced at being worthy to suffer, when I experience unkindness or criticism, I often feel unworthy—that somehow I must have deserved to be punished. Upon reflection, I am likely to think that if only I had said or done things differently, I would have been spared the pain I am feeling.

On the other hand, there have been a few joyful times of "suffering for righteousness" when I did not doubt that I had done exactly what Jesus wanted me to do. The apostles certainly did not look forward to suffering any more than we do, but they rejoiced because they were completely surrendered to God's will, and they evaluated their behavior not by man's opinion but by obedience to their Lord. In fact, surrendering to the lordship of Jesus is essential if we are to appreciate the challenges that come with being a "minister of reconciliation."

What Is Lordship?

What does Jesus' lordship really mean? When we are baptized, confessing "Jesus is Lord" (Romans 10:9), we submit to him in every aspect of our lives—our relationships, career, future plans, personal righteousness, schedule, money and the choices we make throughout each day. We allow him to rule over us—to be our Savior and Lord. There are many folks claiming to be Christians who have never really made Jesus their Lord. Notice how Peter interjects "set apart Christ as Lord" in the middle of the following passage about effective evangelism:

> But even if you should suffer for what is right, you are blessed. "Do not

> fear what they fear; do not be frightened." But in your hearts set apart Christ as Lord. Always be prepared to give an answer to everyone who asks you to give the reason for the hope that you have. But do this with gentleness and respect, keeping a clear conscience, so that those who speak maliciously against your good behavior in Christ may be ashamed of their slander. (1 Peter 3:14–16)

Although cowardice has been a huge struggle for me, when I am making Jesus Lord of everything I think, say and do, I find that I want to share what he is doing in my life, and I am much more likely to open my mouth and share the Good News even if I am frightened or intimidated. Paul tells the Corinthians:

> The weapons we fight with are not the weapons of the world. On the contrary, they have divine power to demolish strongholds. We demolish arguments and every pretension that sets itself up against the knowledge of God, and we take captive every thought to make it obedient to Christ. (2 Corinthians 10:4–5)

"Taking captive every thought" is making Jesus Lord of our thoughts, allowing him to encourage us with faithful, hopeful thoughts, and at the same time preventing Satan from telling us his lies that "you'll never measure up" or "no one loves you—not even God."

But we cannot expect God's help if we are not obeying him. That is why staying in the Word each day is so critical. The more we obey God and surrender to his will as revealed in the Scriptures, the more God will work in our lives to uplift us and give us victories. In the following passage, Jesus affirms the connection between loving God, obeying him and being assured of his support and help in every situation:

> "If you love me, obey my commandments. And I will ask the Father, and he will give you another Advocate, who will never leave you. He is the Holy Spirit, who leads into all truth. The world cannot receive

> him, because it isn't looking for him and doesn't recognize him. But you know him, because he lives with you now and later will be in you. No, I will not abandon you as orphans—I will come to you.
>
> "Soon the world will no longer see me, but you will see me. Since I live, you also will live. When I am raised to life again, you will know that I am in my Father, and you are in me, and I am in you. Those who accept my commandments and obey them are the ones who love me. And because they love me, my Father will love them. And I will love them and reveal myself to each of them." (John 14:15–21, NLT)

Jesus Will Reveal Himself

Do you need more faith to really believe this? Notice the very last line: Jesus says he will reveal himself to us. The more I obey and allow him to work his miracles in and through me, the more faith I have. Then I know, without a doubt, that God did it all, and that I was just a willing participant.

Go back to your Bible and read John 14:12–14, the verses just preceding the passage above. Jesus says we will do even greater things than he did. What could he possibly mean by this? Maybe he was thinking that there would be thousands of us, all allowing his Spirit to work in us throughout the world! While on earth Jesus limited himself to the body of a single man; in going back to the Father and sending his Spirit, he is living in the lives of all his followers. Jesus may be speaking here of the impact he can make through us.

Not only can we reconcile people with God, we can also help his children be reconciled with each other. My husband and I often counsel couples whose marriages are in trouble. Since these people claim to be Bible-believing disciples of Jesus, we would expect them to enjoy harmonious relationships—including a happy marriage. But still they struggle to love each other, to forgive each other, to practice in their most important relationship what they say they believe. Why?

What Prevents Connection?

There is one sin that can prevent us from connecting with God and with other people, one sin that can make it impossible to love as God intends. Can you guess what this sin is? (If you are thinking it is probably some type of sexual sin, you are wrong.)

Notice I said it is a sin that can prevent us from connecting—not a sin that will necessarily destroy positive relationships. This is a sin we all suffer from, but the more we are aware of our struggle, the more we are able to love while praying and working to change.

The sin I am talking about is pride—the kind of pride that thinks, "I'm right—and you should admit it!" In one powerful passage, Paul addresses the problem of pride and the impact it has on the church fellowship, our friendships, marriages and families:

> Is there any encouragement from belonging to Christ? Any comfort from his love? Any fellowship together in the Spirit? Are your hearts tender and compassionate? Then make me truly happy by agreeing wholeheartedly with each other, loving one another, and working together with one mind and purpose.
>
> Don't be selfish; don't try to impress others. Be humble, thinking of others as better than yourselves. Don't look out only for your own interests, but take an interest in others, too.
>
> You must have the same attitude that Christ Jesus had.
>
> Though he was God, he did not think of equality with God as something to cling to. Instead, he gave up his divine privileges; he took the humble position of a slave and was born as a human being. When he appeared in human form, he humbled himself in obedience to God and died a criminal's death on a cross. (Philippians 2:1–8, NLT)

In a word, this passage is about achieving unity, the ability to work and live together, as Paul says, "with one mind and purpose." God made us very different, with a variety of needs, perspectives, personalities and desires. Humility is the only way we can merge our differences into a unified whole, so that our diversity becomes an opportunity, not an obstacle. Yes, great communication skills are helpful, but it is really humility that makes connecting with other people possible in the first place.

In my book, *Catching the Wave of Workforce Diversity,* I wrote:

> Studies show that diverse work groups, properly managed, outperform work groups in which all members are of the same gender and culture.... Employees must learn to be effective even when their customers and coworkers are different from themselves.[2]

Diversity is not just about racial and ethnic issues, it is about any situation where people must communicate despite their different opinions and priorities. One synonym for the word "culture" is "experience." In that sense, we all come from diverse cultures since our personal experiences are very different. In the book I introduce three "keys to intercultural communication"—caring, cultural awareness and communication skills. Humility stems from the first of these keys: we must care enough about connecting with the other person and preserving (or building) the relationship that we are willing to humble ourselves.

Of course, we Christians call this caring *"love."* Yes, communicating with others who see things differently can be a significant challenge, but thinking of this challenge as an opportunity for personal and spiritual growth makes it more likely that we will be humble enough to really hear the other person's concerns, and then respond to those concerns in a productive way.

In our work with married couples, humility is always a necessary part of reconciliation, but we have found that just telling someone to humble out is usually not very effective. First of all, spouses who are caught up in their pride are not likely to listen to each other or to us. Reading Paul's words in Philippians 2 can be helpful, but one way to inspire a more humble attitude is to explain the consequence of humility. The Bible calls for obedience in this area because (1) God loves us, (2) he wants to bless us, and (3) humility *works* in relationships.

For example, when two people disagree, they often want basically the same thing, although they may have different ways to achieve their goal. Spouses typically want a harmonious marriage and a home environment that will be beneficial to their children.

I often share the following analogy with the spouses: parents are like a stereo system, and their children like the speakers, playing out the parents' issues. If parents are angry, even when their anger is under the surface, the children are often sullen and irritable, or act out in explosions of rage. If the parents are deceiving each other (having a secret extramarital affair, for example), the teacher may report that little Amy has trouble telling the truth.

What is amazing is that these patterns are seen even in very young children: even when Mom has tried to "protect" the kids from her true feelings toward Dad, little Frankie senses how Mom really feels and acts it out. (It is also common for children to develop severe behavior problems when they fear an impending divorce. Mom and Dad realize that they will have to pull together to resolve the child's problem so they will stop fighting, at least for a while. Hopefully this will get their attention and move them to true reconciliation.)

The work of reconciliation—whether it is with God or another person—takes a major commitment of time and energy. We must be ready to invest our hearts and lives in relationship-building activities, multiple meetings, and periods of prayer and fasting. We also risk the possibility of heartbreak if our non-Christian friends ultimately decide to walk away. Even Jesus could not persuade everyone: when I am disappointed, I remember how the rich young man was not willing to exchange his worldly wealth for spiritual riches so "he went away sad" (Matthew 19:16–22).

But when our work is rewarded with a new soul added to God's kingdom—or a relationship healed—what joy we experience! All the regrets and disappointments become a dim memory while we celebrate with God's angels.

For More Reflection

1. In 1 Corinthians 9:19, Paul says he "makes himself a slave to win as many as possible." Who are you willing to serve? Reflect in your journal on your thoughts and feelings about making yourself a slave.

2. Are you finding time for evangelism? Find some friends from church, and make a plan to encourage each other and work together to help someone become a Christian.

3. Paul writes, "For God did not give us a spirit of timidity, but a spirit of power, of love and of self-discipline" (2 Timothy 1:7). Which best describes you—a spirit of timidity or a spirit of power, love and self-discipline? If you tend to be more timid, what will your repentance look like? (What are the sins that are keeping you from being more powerful?)

❄

What does Jesus say of the peacemakers? They will be called God's children. What an incredible prediction and promise—but not surprising considering the placement of this beatitude, which comes after developing a pure heart.

Of course this is intentional. Only when we have a heart like Jesus—his humility, his ability to see and mourn the devastation of sin, his meekness, his wholehearted compassion and his holiness—are we able to imitate the Prince of Peace and call his people back into a unified relationship with himself and with others. This heart now prepares us for the next chapter—the final step in our spiritual journey together.

9

Sacrificial Spirit

Reflect the Heart of Christ

"Blessed are those who are persecuted because of righteousness, for theirs is the kingdom of heaven."

Matthew 5:10

This chapter is about suffering, or more accurately, the readiness to follow wherever Jesus leads and, as necessary, to be "persecuted because of righteousness." Throughout this project, as I wrote each chapter, my need to grow in that area became clear. Then God would provide opportunities for me to practice what I was learning.

I am in awe of how God has worked at molding my character. This book has been a journey of amazing spiritual growth for me. Although evangelism has been the most challenging area in my Christian walk, I find myself embracing my role as a "minister of reconciliation" in bolder, more spontaneous ways.

Of course, being evangelistic means we will be viewed not only as "peacemakers" but also as "troublemakers," which is probably why Jesus now talks about blessing in persecution. As Thomas Jones writes in *No One Like Him*,

> Having described the uncommon heart and attitudes the kingdom person will have, Jesus ends on a note of pure realism. If you live like this, people will not like it. Ironically, I suspect it is particularly the peacemaker part that will get us into the most trouble. Most people would be fine if we would practice our own relationship with God and live our own separate lives in humility before him. But that seventh beatitude is where the rub comes. It is when a kingdom person goes forth

> to call others to the kingdom that the offense occurs.
>
> There is a certain irony in the fact that being a peacemaker is what will get you hated, abused, maybe even killed. Jesus was the Prince of Peace. He came to reconcile people to God. Later he would say, "If they persecuted me, they will persecute you also" (John 15:20). Most people just don't want to be disturbed. But there are open hearts out there and in order to find them, we have to go to all kinds of people. We must trust that God will be with us and rejoice that we have found the kingdom—regardless of how others may treat us.[1]

As I begin to write about this eighth and final beatitude, I feel inadequate: Has God spared me from suffering because I have not been righteous or because I have not been willing? Am I really ready now to suffer for my faith?

How will you answer these questions? What about the most important questions of all: Do you absolutely trust God's love and protection? Are you certain that, even in the midst of suffering, you will experience his presence, and that whatever happens, he will never abandon you? Our answers will determine how we respond to God, who is calling each of us to find joy in unquestioning obedience, to...

Reflect the Heart of Christ

Jesus cared only about pleasing his Heavenly Father and doing God's will. Is this your heart? As in the old song, most of us prefer to say, "I did it my way!" and feel that self-sacrifice is a burden. Jesus never sought personal glory or status. He was willing to do anything, to go to any length to glorify his Father and advance the kingdom. Moreover, he found great joy in doing exactly what his Father wanted:

> "If you obey my commands, you will remain in my love, just as I have obeyed my Father's commands and remain in his love. I have told you

> this so that my joy may be in you and that your joy may be complete. My command is this: Love each other as I have loved you." (John 15:10–12)

How I wish I were more like this! How can I grow to have a heart like Jesus—to be wholeheartedly devoted to advancing the kingdom regardless of the personal risks? How can I be passionate about ensuring that every person I meet can know the blessings I have enjoyed as a daughter of the Living God?

Our last three steps involve rejoicing in how far we have come and continuing to grow in our ability to be even more like Jesus:

- Rejoice in Wisdom: Jesus has revealed to us the secrets that enable us not just to exist, but to truly live.
- Rejoice in Persecution: We can fully experience the power and joy of Jesus' resurrection in every aspect of our lives—if we are also willing to share in his suffering and death.
- Rejoice in Expectation: The hope of heaven is more wonderful than we can fathom, and if we suffer righteously during this life, God will use even that to shower us with blessings.

Having climbed almost to the pinnacle on this spiritual ladder of self-awareness and growth, we know that, even as we reach the top, God will continue to transform us until we are perfectly suited for the work of his Holy Spirit. But first let us acknowledge all that God has already done.

Step 1: Rejoice in Wisdom

> Jesus answered, "I am the way and the truth and the life. No one comes to the Father except through me. If you really knew me, you would know my Father as well. From now on, you do know him and have seen him." (John 14:6–7)

Do you realize what Jesus is saying? He is everything we need: the Living Word, the Wisdom of the ages, the Key to the kingdom, the Pearl of great price. And he is ours: our Friend, Companion, Guide, Lord, Savior, the Source of every blessing. He has already given us immeasurably more than all we ask or imagine (Ephesians 3:20).

You would think the apostles reacted to this revelation with immense gratitude and praise! But no. Instead, Philip responds, "Lord, show us the Father and that will be enough for us" (John 14:8). They still didn't get it! (Let us be patient with ourselves if we are also slow to grasp his meaning.) Was Jesus tempted to become frustrated with them? Was he tempted to question himself—to wonder what he might have done to make them understand? No, Jesus simply used this as another opportunity to teach them.

As a psychologist, people sometimes look to me for answers. And I do have the answer: his name is Jesus! Unfortunately, though, that is not always the answer people want. They think that there must be something more, some magic key to happiness. Well, there is—his name is Jesus.

Jesus has given us the Way to thrive, the Truth to stand on, and the Life to celebrate and share. The scientists and scholars in the world know nothing if they do not know Jesus. Do you understand what I am saying? We are the wise ones because we know the secret! (Actually, it is not our wisdom at all—without God we would be as stupid as sheep, but he has given us the secret because we are his beloved children.) Is this a reason to rejoice? You bet it is!

What does God expect from us in return? He provides the key to a life of great blessing and meaning—a life of joy! There must be something God wants. Harvard professor and priest Brendan Manning once said, "In essence, there is only one thing God asks of us—that we be people for whom God is everything and for whom God is enough."

Read this quote again. Does it describe you? Our eyes see all that the world has to offer, and we want, want, want. The thing is, though, that we do not need anything except our God (2 Peter 1:3). Our lives are perfect just as they are. Now that is a reason to rejoice (if we truly believe it). But what if I have challenging relationships, unresolved hurts, physical pain, financial worries, rebellious children, a distant marriage, an insensitive boss? These are the "troubles" Jesus talks about:

> "I have told you these things, so that in me you may have peace. In this world you will have trouble. But take heart! I have overcome the world." (John 16:33)

Response to Difficulties

The question is: What do we do with all these troubles? Someone might say, "It's awesome that Jesus overcomes the world—but tell me how to live my difficult life while I'm waiting for him to whisk me away!" Paul gives us the following advice:

> Therefore we do not lose heart. Though outwardly we are wasting away, yet inwardly we are being renewed day by day. For our light and momentary troubles are achieving for us an eternal glory that far outweighs them all. So we fix our eyes not on what is seen, but on what is unseen. For what is seen is temporary, but what is unseen is eternal. (2 Corinthians 4:16–18)

Basically, Paul says, "Adjust your focus! Keep your eyes fixed on Jesus!" (Also see Hebrews 12:2.) What would Jesus do in my situation? How would he react? What did he say about how to handle this kind of problem? What can I learn from the great heroes of Scripture—Abraham, Joseph, David, Isaiah, Daniel, Peter, Paul?

This is where we find all the wisdom we need. If we build our lives on the rock of his word, we will have God's answers to everything from the tiniest irritations to the most gigantic boulders that seem to completely block our path and prevent us from moving forward (Matthew 7:24–27). Does this inspire me to rejoice? You bet it does!

For More Reflection

1. Think about the fact that you have the secrets that people everywhere are seeking: the Way to be blessed, the Truth about life's meaning, and the Life that really counts. Take a moment right now to praise and thank God for his wonderful gifts.

2. Does your gratitude inspire you to want to share these secrets with someone? Write in your journal about how you will "come into the light" and start sharing the amazing life that Jesus provides.

3. Develop a Bible study plan that will give you more complete access to God's answers for life's practical challenges. In a notebook, list the difficulties you or your friends have faced recently, leaving space to note God's answers. Then spend some time each day searching God's word for perspective and solutions to these life challenges. This notebook then becomes a handy resource for overcoming life's hurdles and for giving friends spiritual input.

Step 2: Rejoice in Persecution

I want to know Christ and experience the mighty power that raised him from the dead. I want to suffer with him, sharing in his death, so that one way or another I will experience the resurrection from the dead!

I don't mean to say that I have already achieved these things or that I have already reached perfection. But I press on to possess that perfection for which Christ Jesus first possessed me. No, dear broth-

> ers and sisters, I have not achieved it, but I focus on this one thing: Forgetting the past and looking forward to what lies ahead, I press on to reach the end of the race and receive the heavenly prize for which God, through Christ Jesus, is calling us. (Philippians 3:10–14, NLT)

Paul inspires me to r…e…a…c…h for greater faith and higher levels of spiritual experience. Paul was a Pharisee who went about persecuting Christians, but then Christ "possessed" him and his life would never be the same. This is interesting language: we speak of someone being "possessed" by a demon, but if Christ is living in and through us, we are possessed by Christ. Christ owns us and gives us a new heart and spirit—his own Spirit—so we will eagerly do God's work (even if it means suffering) because we love him that much.

This is why Paul was able to say, "I no longer live, but Christ lives in me" (Galatians 2:20). His whole reason and method for living, his whole life, became about Christ and, as much as possible, achieving that perfection to which Jesus is calling us (Matthew 5:48). Paul says he wants to "know" Christ—to become one with him. He understood that the only way to experience Christ's resurrection power in his own life was to be fully united with Christ and allow the Spirit of Christ to live in him.

We must be willing to share in Christ's death if we are to experience Christ's resurrection life:

> Jesus replied, "The hour has come for the Son of Man to be glorified. I tell you the truth, unless a kernel of wheat falls to the ground and dies, it remains only a single seed. But if it dies, it produces many seeds. The man who loves his life will lose it, while the man who hates his life in this world will keep it for eternal life." (John 12:23–25)

Do you want to experience the power and joy of Christ? Then you must be willing to "die" to your sins, your selfish interests and needs. We are called each day to carry our own cross of suffering and death so we can enjoy the true life that Jesus offers. Jesus knew how hard it would be for us to openly share about him—and how that kind of openness would bring humiliation and persecution. As true disciples of Jesus, this is the kind of daily "death" we must accept (and, if necessary, a physical death as well: Luke 9:23–26).

How can we begin to compare this kind of suffering to what Jesus suffered for us? Is Jesus asking a lot? Not when we consider the kind of death he died for us.

Being Like Christ

This chapter is called "Reflect the Heart of Christ." The more we know Christ and share his heart—his character, motives, passions—the more willing and eager we will be to go anywhere, give up anything or suffer in any way to advance his kingdom. And because we have his power, the more we will be able to perform "miracles" (although actually it will be Christ living in us).

Of course our motives are important. If, like Simon the Sorcerer (Acts 8:9–24), we follow Christ for personal gain, God will not bless our efforts, no matter how much we suffer.

How can we grow to know Jesus and share his heart? Again, time in his word is the answer. John 1:1 tells us that "in the beginning was the Word, and the Word was with God and the Word was God." Then, in verse 14: "The Word became flesh and made his dwelling among us." Clearly, the more we immerse ourselves in Scripture, the better we will know Christ and become one with him.

But how can we rejoice in persecution? The theme of Paul's letter to the believers at Philippi exemplifies being joyful in the worst of circumstances. Here is just a sampling of verses from the New Living Translation of chapter 1:

> You share with me the special favor of God, both in my imprisonment and in defending and confirming the truth of the Good News. (Philippians 1:7b)

> Whether their motives are false or genuine, the message about Christ is being preached either way, so I rejoice. And I will continue to rejoice. (Philippians 1:18b)

> For you have been given not only the privilege of trusting in Christ but also the privilege of suffering for him. (Philippians 1:29)

First, Paul talks about being blessed by God even in prison. Verse 18 explains that he will rejoice as long as Christ is preached. And finally, he speaks of the "privilege" of suffering for Christ. What faith! How did he do it? In a familiar verse, Paul answers that question:

> For I can do everything through Christ, who gives me strength. (Philippians 4:13)

Because this verse is so often quoted, we can miss the meaning behind it. Paul is basically saying that Christ is the prism through which his entire life flows. Rather than self-reliance, he practiced Christ-reliance. Christ influenced and, in fact, controlled everything he did and everything he was.

Paul knew that evangelism could bring persecution, but even so, he believed that sharing our faith increases our awareness and appreciation of God's blessings:

> I pray that you may be active in sharing your faith, so that you will have a full understanding of every good thing we have in Christ. (Philemon 6)

For More Reflection

1. Answer the following questions in your journal: In what ways are you "possessed by Christ"? In what ways are you still self-reliant? How will you surrender to God more fully?

2. In what ways are you "carrying your cross" each day, dying to your sins, your selfishness, desire for approval from people, your worldliness?

3. Have you been persecuted for your faith? How can you grow to be bolder and more effective in your evangelism?

Step 3: Rejoice in Expectation

> Since everything here today might well be gone tomorrow, do you see how essential it is to live a holy life? Daily expect the Day of God, eager for its arrival. The galaxies will burn up and the elements melt down that day—but we'll hardly notice. We'll be looking the other way, ready for the promised new heavens and the promised new earth, all landscaped with righteousness.
>
> So, my dear friends, since this is what you have to look forward to, do your very best to be found living at your best, in purity and peace. (2 Peter 3:11–14, The Message)

Eager anticipation is one of the great blessings of life. We look forward to holidays, vacations, reunions with family and old friends, and just having time to relax. How dreary life would be without these special events! People suffering from depression often perceive that they have nothing to look forward to, that they will never experience relief from the burdens of life.

Peter says that, as Christians, we look forward to the "day of God." We will be with God for the vast years of eternity, and our current difficulties will be a distant memory. Yesterday I heard that the Hubble telescope just discovered a galaxy that is 12.8 billion years old. It is roughly 2.2 billion light-years away, which means that we are seeing what it looked like 2.2 billion light-years ago (and a light-year—the distance light travels in a year—is 5,878,625,373,183.61 miles!)

Another astonishing tidbit: this newly-discovered galaxy is 2,000 light-years wide. Not only are these numbers beyond my comprehension, but my life seems very small and insignificant in comparison. Here is the incredible thing though: My life is not insignificant at all to God! Our wonderful Father created all that exists many eons ago, but he still knows (and cares about) the number of hairs on my little head (Matthew 10:30).

Eternity will be longer than countless billions of light-years, and that is how long we will be with God. So what if we have struggles now? They are less than a "drop in the bucket" when we consider eternity. So Peter cautions us not to throw away eternity because we are too sinful or lazy to care about being righteous.

Jesus promises in this beatitude that if our righteousness results in persecution, we are still rewarded with the kingdom of heaven. Paul makes a similar claim:

> Now if we are children, then we are heirs—heirs of God and co-heirs with Christ, if indeed we share in his sufferings in order that we may also share in his glory. (Romans 8:17)

We have a heavenly inheritance. As God's beneficiaries, we stand to inherit exceedingly more than a child of the wealthiest tycoon. I am amazed at the lengths to which reality show contestants will go to win moderately large sums of money. They eat live insects (supposedly an exotic delicacy), compete in activities that would terrify the most experienced stuntmen, immerse their bodies in tubs of crawling worms and make complete fools of themselves on national television—just for the possibility of winning a million dollars. But all we have to do to receive an eternally valuable inheritance is continue to trust God, living in obedience to his word and allowing his Holy Spirit to have complete reign over us.

What About Now?

Yes, we have much to anticipate after death, but what about now? God promises that he has plans to prosper us, to give us hope and a future (Jeremiah 29:11). He also promises that our suffering will not be in vain:

> Not only so, but we also rejoice in our sufferings, because we know that suffering produces perseverance; perseverance, character; and character, hope. (Romans 5:3–4)

Suffering caused by sin is meaningless, but when we suffer righteously, God uses that pain to bring about something beautiful: afterwards, we are stronger and more fully equipped to do his will so he can bring us even more blessing. There have been times I have survived a painful experience but later appreciated that with God on my side, I was stronger than I had known. The realization that I could survive—and thrive—through future challenges then brought me great hope and increased confidence.

Before Adam was baptized into Christ he had hit a wall in his Bible studies, and for a time everyone was unsure whether he would continue. My first reaction was to try to "force" him to accept the truth. But the harder I pushed, the more he pushed back.

Frustrated and frightened, I remember going out one morning and sitting by a lake, where I cried and poured out my desperate prayers that God would change Adam's heart. Then I promised God that, even though I could not imagine going on without Adam by my side spiritually, no matter what happened, I would remain faithful until the very end. I chose to leave the matter with God, knowing that he wanted Adam to "make it" even more than I did.

A few days later, the men studying with Adam told me he had resolved his doubts and would be committing himself to Jesus in baptism that Sunday. Looking back, I believe God was testing my unconditional commitment. Today Adam serves the church as an elder, thanks to our marvelous and gracious God.

Peter writes:

> And the God of all grace, who called you to his eternal glory in Christ, after you have suffered a little while, will himself restore you and make you strong, firm and steadfast. (1 Peter 5:10)

When viewed in this light, getting older is definitely a blessing. How many times have I heard people say, "I wish I'd known then what I know now"? It is no wonder that teens have such a difficult time. Like birds leaving the nest, they have just begun to venture out into dangerous terrain without the awareness and strength that comes with maturity.

Getting older may mean a few extra aches and inches, but as disciples of Jesus, it also means we are closer to being with God. That is why it is sobering to think about aging without the assurance of heaven. Many elderly people either do not realize the cause of their emptiness or, even if they are able to identify its spiritual roots, they may not have access to a spiritual mentor who can guide them toward the Truth.

So, rather than turn to God for healing, some opt for unhealthy addictions to numb out, or even choose to prematurely end their lives. This may explain the incidence of suicide among men over seventy-five, which is roughly twice that of other adult men.

Using Gifts for God

Although thinking about old age and suicide may seem morbid, this is the tragic reality. But for us, there is good news: getting older can mean getting better! Maturity can yield wisdom and reliance on God, along with an increased ability to use our gifts as he intended. Of course, the key here is "as he intended."

In my selfish ambition I may strive to do something important or exceptional with my gifts and talents, but God will determine what I can actually achieve—and that is good enough for me (Proverbs 16:9).

Jesus was the Lord of Lords—God's only Son, yet he "made himself nothing and took the humble position of a slave" (Philippians 2:7, NLT). At the beginning of his ministry, though, he was tempted to exalt himself and seek personal power (Luke 4:5–7).

Likewise, many of us are tempted in our heart of hearts with a desire for personal recognition, all the while knowing that our goal must be to glorify Christ. So God in his infinite mercy ordains that when we share in Christ's sufferings we will also share in his glory (Romans 8:17).

This is a promise to cherish as we carry the cross of sacrificial service. Our wonderful Lord has indeed thought of everything, and he truly meets all our needs. What more is there to say? Only this:

> ...faith and love...spring from the hope that is stored up for you in heaven and that you have already heard about in the word of truth, the gospel that has come to you. (Colossians 1:5–6)

Through the Scriptures we find the things that endure—faith, love and hope—and thus *discover* the joy of Christ.

For More Reflection

1. What are you looking forward to? Take some special time to thank God for all the hopes and dreams he has planted in your heart.

2. Paul said, "I press on toward the goal to win the prize for which God has called me heavenward in Christ Jesus" (Philippians 3:14). What are you willing to do in the "reality show" of your own life to win the heavenly prize?

3. How are you getting better with each year? How can you pass on to the next generation the lessons you have learned and life skills you have gained (see Titus 2)?

❄

What does Jesus say of those who are persecuted? "Theirs is the kingdom of heaven." Does this sound familiar? Jesus began his

Beatitudes with a similar statement, promising that the kingdom of heaven belongs to those who are poor in spirit. Thus, we have come full circle.

The more I grow in each of these foundational principles, the more God shows me my need to go right back to the beginning, so that my life in Christ literally revolves around him and his wonderful word. All the while he is planting and watering, cultivating his fruit in my character, as we will see in our final chapter.

10

Now Taste the Spirit's Fruit

But the fruit of the Spirit is love, joy, peace, patience, kindness, goodness, faithfulness, gentleness and self-control. Against such things there is no law.

Galatians 5:22–23

We all wish for these qualities that Paul calls the fruit of the Spirit, and they only emanate from a life lived in obedience to, filled with, and under the control of the Holy Spirit. Obedience is a conscious act of humble submission, but the "filling" is a gift given by God in response to our obedience, which first occurs when we repent of our sin and surrender our lives in the water of baptism (Acts 2:38).

Thereafter, with each moment that we yield to him, God gives us more and more of his power according to our need. With time and maturity, self-will is gradually fused with his will, so that eventually the life is "not I but Christ" (Galatians 2:20). In essence, this is vibrant mental health—a life that is completely surrendered to God and able to experience his wonderful fruit.

Not only are the Beatitudes the "greenhouse" that enables his fruit to blossom, but they are the perfect diagnostic tool or method for assessing the reasons why we are not filled with joy. Of course, my colleagues in the profession of psychology may consider me a "heretic" with such a radical statement. Back in the 1970s I wrote in my journal that "Jesus was the first psychologist," and three decades later this is still my conviction.

Fruit of the Spirit: Beatitudes

Before we discuss how to use the diagnostic tool included in this chapter, let us look at the fruit that might sprout from each progressive step we have discussed in this book.

Love

Spiritual Poverty: Deciding to be Wholehearted

When we see and fully accept our insufficiency—how desperately we need God's forgiveness and daily help—a reasonable response is to decide, once and for all, to love God with all our heart, soul, mind and strength. Only then are we able to obey Jesus' second commandment: to love others as we love ourselves (Mark 12:30–31).

Loving God and loving other people are inseparable. If we are not loving with people, this shows that we do not love God since it is more difficult to love someone we have never seen (1 John 4:20). Also, loving people is evidence that we do love God, as John says in the following passage:

> Dear friends, let us continue to love one another, for love comes from God. Anyone who loves is a child of God and knows God. But anyone who does not love does not know God, for God is love. (1 John 4:7–8, NLT)

Although this sounds like a "chicken and egg" problem, deciding to love God and seek him wholeheartedly comes first, since love is a fruit of his Spirit. The more surrendered we are to him, the more we will realize the residency of his Spirit in our lives, and the more loving we will be. It may not be rational to love those who hate or mistreat us, but this is the work of the Holy Spirit—and this is what sets us apart from those who do not have the Spirit.

Patience

Contrition: Imagining God's Comfort

Although mourning our sin may not be a pleasant emotional experience, it is essential if we are to be patient with others. I can only accept the failings of my brother when I fully acknowledge my own. Recently I had a painful experience with a non-Christian who was more than insensitive or nasty; it seemed she was "out to get me." I struggled with how I could love my enemy, as Jesus commanded. Thinking about how I would be without God—how unhappy and bitter I could become—has helped me pray for, understand and accept her, despite the pain she has caused me.

Even when we are aware of our own sinful nature, being patient can be challenging. When we have communicated our expectations to spouses or children again and again with little or no response, we can become impatient. We become impatient with those who continue to complain about their circumstances but are still slow to change after being shown how they are contributing to the problem. We can even become impatient with other drivers who act as if they have the only car on the road.

That is why continual confession and repentance are so important—this is not a one-time thing for new Christians, but an act that helps keep us aware of who we are, and who we would be without God's grace.

Peace

Meekness: Surrendering to God

I have noticed that stress and anxiety often fill my heart when I am not surrendered. On the other hand, when I trust that God is good to his word, that he will never leave or forsake me (Deuteronomy 31:6), then I am more able to accept whatever comes along with a peaceful, serene heart.

Meekness also helps me be at peace with other people. Although my intentions are benevolent, I am naturally inclined to try to control the behavior of other people by persuading, rescuing or even manipulating. But surrender makes us willing to give other people freedom to make their own decisions and mistakes. Of course this takes faith. With Paul I must be able to say, "I know the one in whom I trust, and I am sure that he is able to guard what I have entrusted to him" (2 Timothy 1:12b, NLT).

Faithfulness

Hunger: Committing to Spiritual Growth

As emphasized throughout this book, God's word is the key to spiritual growth:

> But as for you, continue in what you have learned and have become convinced of, because you know those from whom you learned it, and how from infancy you have known the holy Scriptures, which are able to make you wise for salvation through faith in Christ Jesus. All Scripture is God-breathed and is useful for teaching, rebuking, correcting and training in righteousness, so that the man of God may be thoroughly equipped for every good work. (2 Timothy 3:14–17)

This is true, not because we learn concepts (as we might from the Internet or a magazine) but because the Scriptures are living and active (Hebrews 4:12–13). Through them, the Holy Spirit does his supernatural work, and the result is much more than passive faith. This fruit involves increased faithfulness and devotion—unwavering, enduring faith in action.

This is the faith practiced by Enoch, Abraham and Sarah, Jacob, Joseph and the other heroes of Hebrews 11. It is also the kind of faith that will enable us to live in a way that honors God and results in great blessing and joy.

Kindness

Mercy: Overflowing with Compassion

On the surface this one seems, to quote a popular expression, like a no-brainer. Biblical kindness and mercy usually go hand in hand, and in fact are almost synonymous. For example, while the following scripture refers to the angels' kindness in the New International Version, notice how the New King James Version translates the word "kindness" as "mercy":

> "Your servant has found favor in your eyes, and you have shown great kindness to me in sparing my life. But I can't flee to the mountains; this disaster will overtake me, and I'll die." (Genesis 19:19, NIV)

> "Indeed now, your servant has found favor in your sight, and you have increased your mercy which you have shown me by saving my life; but I cannot escape to the mountains, lest some evil overtake me and I die." (Genesis 19:19, NKJV)

However, our culture sees little difference between being kind and being nice. Consider this: Are you a "nice person" when treated well but, when subjected to unfair treatment, react in a way that is very unmerciful?

Many people would even say it is unreasonable to be kind to those who are mean-spirited or hateful. Jesus' standards are simply a lot more rigorous. His yardstick for kindness is tailor-made for times when human imperfections are exposed—when someone commits a faux pas, says something insensitive or hurts our feelings. Are we able to be merciful in these moments?

This is much more difficult than being kind to those who treat us with gentleness, but it is what differentiates those who walk with the Spirit and those who attempt to walk in their own power.

Goodness

Purity: Valuing Holiness

"Good" is one of those words we toss around but has lost much of its meaning. We speak of eating good pizza, visiting a good discount store, buying a good pair of jeans, finding a good man and even having a good cry. These expressions have very little to do with God's definition of goodness. I used to think I was a "good person," but Jesus said that only God is good (Mark 10:18). Since goodness is a fruit of his Spirit, anything good about us has only come from his grace and work in our lives.

First, how does God define goodness? According to Jesus, we need not guess whether someone is good on the inside; we can simply look and listen:

> "No good tree bears bad fruit, nor does a bad tree bear good fruit. Each tree is recognized by its own fruit. People do not pick figs from thornbushes, or grapes from briers. The good man brings good things out of the good stored up in his heart, and the evil man brings evil things out of the evil stored up in his heart. For out of the overflow of his heart his mouth speaks." (Luke 6:43–45)

The things we say and do reflect the inner heart. But even good hearts do not always get good results. While being questioned by the high priest, as always Jesus spoke truthfully. But an official standing nearby struck him anyway, because he did not like what Jesus had said (John 18:22). The more we grow to be like God, the more we can expect to be opposed by Satan's forces of darkness.

The important question, though, is how we get good hearts in the first place. Does valuing purity and personal holiness result in goodness? In view of the following passages, the answer is a resounding "Yes!":

> But if we walk in the light, as he is in the light, we have fellowship with one another, and the blood of Jesus, his Son, purifies us from all sin. (1 John 1:7)

> For you were once darkness, but now you are light in the Lord. Live as children of light (for the fruit of the light consists in all goodness, righteousness and truth). (Ephesians 5:8–9)

In other words, when we care enough about personal holiness to openly confess our temptation and sin, Jesus purifies us and, as a result, we grow in goodness.

Gentleness

Peacemaking: Encouraging Reconciliation

The longer I am a disciple of Jesus, the more convinced I am that gentleness is an essential attribute for those who want to practice reconciliation. Many of us, as young Christians, were full of zeal, but in our enthusiasm tried to force faith on those who were cautiously approaching God. In so doing, we only succeeded in pushing them away.

Elijah had been a passionate servant of God, but had become disheartened, fearful and in desperate need of encouragement. How did God get Elijah moving again? Did he rebuke Elijah in a thundering voice? Did he reveal himself in a powerful wind? In a roaring fire? An earthquake? No, God came to Elijah in a gentle whisper (1 Kings 19:1–18).

As I help restore the faith of those who have served God in the past, I am constantly learning that it is God who does the work of reconciliation. I may come prepared with what I consider an inspired plan and "just the right Scriptures," but then God reveals his plan. The more gentle and humble I am (and the more "I" stay out of the way), the more God can do his miraculous work to restore a heart. The bottom line? As I encourage reconciliation, God is teaching me gentleness.

Self-Control

A Sacrificial Spirit: Reflecting the Heart of Christ

Self-control is about resisting one's natural inclination. If totally unrestrained, most of us would choose the Epicurean philosophies of "live for the moment," and "eat, drink and be merry." Self-control is being able to say "no" to myself, reining in my tendency toward complete selfishness.

I have always thought this was a strange New Testament concept, since, as Christians, we must choose to allow God (rather than self) to master us. But the self-control is in the choosing—will I choose God to control me or will I choose something else—whether it is my own sinful nature, other people, or another unhealthy dependency?

In the last chapter we discussed having Christ's heart of unquestioning obedience, being willing and even eager to die to our own selfishness so that God will be glorified. As we refuse to give in to our sinful desires, we must consciously exert some self-control, but the more we choose to walk the Via Dolorosa—Christ's way of suffering—the more the Spirit's fruit of effortless self-control will blossom in our lives.

Joy

The Promise Fulfilled

As we discussed in chapter one, Jesus promised that we will experience joy—the ninth fruit—as we put each beatitude into practice. This is especially true since, at the same time, we will also be growing in the other fruits of his Spirit.

More than ever, I am in awe of seeing myself changing, developing in ways that can only be described as miraculous. Although I have not made a "self-improvement plan" or exerted any superhuman effort, I am becoming more loving, peaceful, patient, kind, good, gentle, faithful and self-controlled. I am definitely not perfect or "there" yet, but I have discovered great joy in this process of growing, as it is clearly due to God's intervention.

This is what God wants to give everyone, and the more I experience it, the more I want to share it. What a perfect motivation for evangelism—to be so full of Jesus' joy that "my cup overflows" and spills over onto the people I meet.

The Beatitudes As a Diagnostic Tool

Now let us return to the idea of using the Beatitudes as a "diagnostic tool." It is important to realize that this is not a "quick fix," since repentance and behavioral change take time as we develop more godly habits. It is also not meant to replace professional psychological help when emotional distress is so severe that it prevents an individual from fulfilling normal life responsibilities or engaging in enjoyable activities.

On the other hand, if you (or others) are feeling discouraged or "stuck," the following questions can be helpful to better understand the problem and then get you moving in a spiritual direction. Answering the questions can be useful in identifying which areas need deeper study, prayer and spiritual focus.

As necessary, go back and read the chapter again, paying special attention to the scriptures referenced and looking for additional scriptures on those topics.

Chapter 2
Decide to Be Wholehearted

1. Who are you relying on—yourself, someone else or God?
2. Do you ask Christian friends for advice?
3. Are you willing to be desperate for God's help, and ready to be vulnerable with God and other Christians?

Chapter 3
Imagine God's Comfort

1. What makes you feel secure? Is it your relationship with God? Or do you get security from something else (being "perfect," getting approval, your talents and skills, etc.)?
2. When was the last time you wrote out a list of your sins, confessed your sins to a trusted friend and sincerely worked on repentance?
3. Are there certain character sins that still plague you? Have you asked for help in overcoming these sins?

Chapter 4
Surrender to God

1. On a scale of one to ten, what is your level of gratitude for all the ways God has intervened in your life to help and protect you in the past?
2. When was the last time you gave up control and really relied on God in a difficult situation? (Or have you found that you try to take charge at those times?)
3. What do you do in the face of crippling fear? Do you fall apart emotionally, or are you able to gain strength from prayer and Scripture?

Chapter 5
Commit to Spiritual Growth

1. What does it feel like to contemplate living life without faith in God?
2. Is your relationship with God cold, lukewarm or hot?
3. Can you name one thing that you could do to heat up your level of devotion?
4. Have you committed scriptures to memory that can help free you from those "negative emotions" that rob you of your joy?

Chapter 6
Overflow with Compassion

1. Do you feel connected to Jesus? Is this always true—or does your feeling of connection come and go depending on your circumstances?

2. Do you feel uncomfortable about facing your weakness head-on?
3. Do you secretly believe that you can do good things even without God's help?
4. Does your prayer life need a boost? Do you need "quantity or quality"—to spend more time in prayer or to achieve a deeper connection to God?

Chapter 7
Value Holiness

1. Are you becoming more and more like Jesus?
2. Do you really believe that God will use you in miraculous ways if you stay close to him?
3. Are you excited about becoming more righteous and useful to God?

Chapter 8
Encourage Reconciliation

1. Does anxiety keep you from enjoying the peace that Jesus promised?
2. Do you feel effective in helping people reconcile with God?
3. What about helping people become more unified with each other?

Chapter 9
Reflect the Heart of Christ

1. How do you react to this statement: "God has given you everything you need"?
2. Are you dying to your selfish nature each day—and loving it?
3. How are you getting "better" as you get older?
4. What unique strengths or skills will you pass on to the younger generation?

Finally, let us take a moment to visit Luke's version of the Beatitudes:

> Looking at his disciples, he said: "Blessed are you who are poor, for yours is the kingdom of God. Blessed are you who hunger now, for you will be satisfied. Blessed are you who weep now, for you will

> laugh. Blessed are you when men hate you, when they exclude you and insult you and reject your name as evil, because of the Son of Man. Rejoice in that day and leap for joy, because great is your reward in heaven. For that is how their fathers treated the prophets.
>
> "But woe to you who are rich, for you have already received your comfort. Woe to you who are well fed now, for you will go hungry. Woe to you who laugh now, for you will mourn and weep. Woe to you when all men speak well of you, for that is how their fathers treated the false prophets." (Luke 6:20–26)

As Jesus' disciples, we are to look different and live differently from the rest of the world. But the sacrifices we make to advance his kingdom cannot be compared with the blessing we experience in this life, and the future blessing in store for us. On the other hand, Jesus warns that if we are unwilling to surrender our lives and instead choose to live for our own comfort and glory, we will miss out on all the joy God gives to those who love him and live for him.

I am so grateful that I am one of the "lucky ones"—that God revealed this to me at a time in my life when I could still choose the best way to live.

❋

As I write these final words, I am moved once more by all the ways God has inspired and blessed me in the process of writing this book. May you also *discover joy* and find the faith, hope and love reserved for you as God's precious child!

> And this is my prayer: that your love may abound more and more in knowledge and depth of insight, so that you may be able to discern what is best and may be pure and blameless until the day of Christ, filled with the fruit of righteousness that comes through Jesus Christ—to the glory and praise of God. (Philippians 1:9–11)

Notes

Chapter 1: The Search for Joy

1. The six-step "UNIQUE" program included the following steps: Understand your past, Nurture your talents, Illuminate your values, Qualify yourself, Unleash your potential, Empower others.

2. J.E. Albino, "Health Psychology and Primary Prevention: Natural Allies," in *Preventive Psychology,* eds. R.D. Felner, L.A. Jason, J.N. Moritsugu, and S.S. Farber (New York: Pergamon, 1983), 221–233.

3. E. Diener, R.E. Lucas, and S. Oishi, "Subjective Well-Being: The Science of Happiness and Life Satisfaction," in *Handbook of Positive Psychology,* eds. C.R. Snyder and S.J. Lopez (New York: Oxford University Press, 2002), 63.

4. C.D. Ryff and C.L.M. Keyes, "The Structure of Psychological Well-Being Revisited," *Journal of Personality and Social Psychology* 69 (1995): 719–727.

5. C.L.M. Keyes, "Social Well-Being," *Social Psychology Quarterly* 61(1998): 121–140.

6. K.I. Pargament and A. Mahoney, "Spirituality: Discovering and Conserving the Sacred," in *Handbook of Positive Psychology,* eds. C.R. Snyder and S.J. Lopez (New York: Oxford University Press, 2002), 654.

7. D.B. Larson, J.P. Swyers and M.E. McCullough, "Scientific Research on Spirituality and Health: A Consensus Report," (Rockville, MD: National Institute for Healthcare Research, 1997).

8. R.A. Emmons, C. Cheung, C. and K. Tehrani, "Assessing Spirituality Through Personal Goals: Implications for Research on Religion and Subjective Well-Being," in *Social Indicators Research* 45 (1998): 391–422.

9. K.I. Pargament, B. Smith, H.G. Koenig and L. Perez, "Patterns of Positive and Negative Religious Coping with Major Life Stressors," in *Journal for the Scientific Study of Religion* 37 (1998): 711–725.

10. J.R. Mickley, K.I. Pargament, C.R. Brand and K.M. Hipp, "God and the Search for Meaning Among Hospice Caregivers," *Hospice Journal* 13 (1998): 1–18.

11. A. Mahoney, K.I. Pargament, T. Jewell, A.B. Swank, C. Scott, E.

Emery and M. Rye, "Marriage and the Spiritual Realm: The Role of Proximal and Distal Religious Constructs in Marital Functioning," *Journal of Family Psychology* 13 (1999): 321–338.

12. A. Swank, A. Mahoney and K.I. Pargament, "The Sanctification of Parenting and Its Psychosocial Implications," Paper presented at the meeting of the Society of the Scientific Study of Religion, Boston (October 1999).

13. M.R. McMinn, *Psychology, Theology, and Spirituality in Christian Counseling* (Carol Stream, IL: Tyndale, 1996), 46.

14. Martin Seligman, *Authentic Happiness* (New York: Simon & Schuster, The Free Press: 2002), 8.

15. C.R. Solomon, *Handbook to Happiness: A Biblical Guide to Victorious Living* (Carol Stream, IL: Tyndale, 1999), 135.

16. E. Stanley Jones, *Growing Spiritually* (New York: Abingdon, 1953), 1.

17. F.C. Thompson, *Thompson Chain Reference Bible* (Indianapolis: B.B. Kirkbride Bible Company, and Grand Rapids: Zondervan, 1983).

18. J.C. Howell, *The Beatitudes for Today* (Louisville: Westminster John Knox Press, 2006), 16.

Chapter 2: Decide to Be Wholehearted

1. Thomas Jones and Michael Fontenot, *The Prideful Soul's Guide to Humility* (Spring Hill, TN: DPI, 1998).

2. Although the Scriptures do provide answers to the normal challenges of living, in some cases feelings of worthlessness can signal a more serious problem that requires professional psychological help. Anyone who experiences the following symptoms for more than two weeks should consider consulting a physician or mental health professional:

- Unintentional weight loss or gain, or a significant change in appetite (especially when combined with one or both of the following)
- Inability to sleep or the desire to sleep all the time
- Thoughts of death or suicide

3. Robin Weidner, *Secure in Heart: Overcoming Insecurity in a Woman's Life* (Spring Hill, TN: DPI, 2006).

4. Gordon Ferguson, *The Victory of Surrender* (Spring Hill, TN: DPI, 1991), 27.

Chapter 3: Imagine God's Comfort

1. Adam Clarke, *The Commentarie* (1825) included in Epiphany Software: Bible Discoverer, 1999.

2. Matthew Henry, *Commentary on the Whole Bible, Unabridged* (1721) included in Epiphany Software: Bible Discoverer, 1999.

3. Mike Leatherwood, Brenda Leatherwood, Declan Joyce and Joanne Randall *Some Sat in Darkness: Spiritual Recovery from Addiction and Codependency* (Spring Hill, TN: DPI, 1997), 107.

4. Gordon Ferguson, *Discipling: God's Plan to Train and Transform His People* (Spring Hill, TN: DPI, 1997—out of print).

5. For a great study of God's plan for relationships in our lives, I recommend Tom Jones and Steve Brown's book *One Another,* published in 2008 by DPI.

Chapter 4: Surrender to God

1. John MacArthur, *The Beatitudes: The Only Way to Happiness* (Chicago: Moody Press, 1980), 97.

2. Rick Warren, *The Purpose Driven Life* (Grand Rapids: Zondervan, 2002).

Chapter 5: Commit to Spiritual Growth

1. Martin Seligman, *Authentic Happiness* (New York: Simon & Schuster, The Free Press: 2002), 8.

Chapter 6: Overflow with Compassion

1. Mark Templer, *The Prayer of the Righteous* (Spring Hill, TN: DPI, 2000), 91–144.

Chapter 7: Value Holiness

1. Gordon Ferguson, *The Power of Spiritual Thinking* (Spring Hill, TN: DPI, 2000—out of print), 8.

2. Thomas Hanks, *For God So Loved the Third World* (Mary Knoll, NY: Orbis Books, 1983).

3. Lowell Noble, "Oppression: Biblical and Experiential," (Jackson, MS: Spencer Perkins Center for Reconciliation and Youth Development, undated paper).

4. Camerin Courtney, "A Higher Calling," *Today's Christian Woman* 24, no. 6 (Nov/Dec 2002): 42.

Chapter 8: Encourage Reconciliation

1. Linda Dillow, *Calm My Anxious Heart* (Colorado Springs: NavPress, 1998), 136.

2. Joy Bodzioch, *Catching the Wave of Workforce Diversity: Powerful New Skills for Managers* (Eugene, OR: BookPartners, 1995), 10.

Chapter 9: Reflect the Heart of Christ

1. Thomas Jones, *No One Like Him* (Spring Hill, TN: DPI, 2002), 109–110.

Other Encouraging Products from DPI Books

Mind Change

A Biblical Path to Overcoming Life's Challenges

Thomas A. Jones

Helps you to transform negative thinking to God-oriented thinking. "Yes" problems..."but" God.

Audio book also available. Check out www.mindchangeonline.org to sign up for weekly podcast by the author.

Rejoice Always

A Handbook for Christians Facing Emotional Challenges

Drs. Michael and Mary Shapiro

Two licensed psychologists, who are disciples, unlock some of the mysteries of mental disorders and provide Biblical answers for those seeking spiritual victory.

www.dpibooks.org

Dare to Dream Again

Getting Back Up When Life Knocks You Down

Jeff Chacon

If you have ever felt knocked down or even knocked out in your faith, this uplifting book will inspire you to never give up your dreams of doing great things for God!

The Victory of Surrender

Gordon Ferguson

Explores crucial biblical principles related to surrender, and lavishly illustrates them with stories from the author's life. This teaching will guide you to "let go" and find real and practical freedom in the sovereign will of God.

www.dpibooks.org